Reginald Fanshaw

Two Lives

A Poem

Reginald Fanshaw

Two Lives
A Poem

ISBN/EAN: 9783744717724

Printed in Europe, USA, Canada, Australia, Japan

Cover: Foto ©Thomas Meinert / pixelio.de

More available books at **www.hansebooks.com**

TWO LIVES

A POEM BY

REGINALD FANSHAWE

LONDON
GEORGE BELL AND SONS
AND NEW YORK
1894

CHISWICK PRESS:—C. WHITTINGHAM AND CO., TOOKS COURT,
CHANCERY LANE.

CONTENTS.

	PAGE
PREFACE	vii
DEDICATION	xv
INTRODUCTION	xxiii

CANTO I.—DEATH. NATURE. SONG.

Winter	3
Spirit of Spring	13
Summer	22
Autumn	33
Song's Dream	46
Love and Song	60
Life and Song	74
Second Spring	83

CANTO II.—DREAM. DOUBT. NATURE.

Twilight	89
Respice	98
Dream and Doubt	110
Song and Life	121
Growth	135
Cui Bono	153
Song's Season	173
Something White	177

PREFACE.

A COMPLETED poem should need neither preface nor apology. A fragment, perhaps, may qualify its imperfections, at least provisionally, by both. The sub-

ERRATA.

Page xviii, stanza 2, line 5, *for* " leave " *read* " give."
Page 175, stanza 1, line 3, *for* " month's " *read* " months."

PREFACE.

A COMPLETED poem should need neither preface nor apology. A fragment, perhaps, may qualify its imperfections, at least provisionally, by both. The subject of this song might best be described as a spiritual pilgrimage from nothingness and denial to hope and fulfilment; as a vision of the progress of life through the experience of nature, self and history, to God.

The note of the poem is primarily *personal*. It presents an authentic record of real individual growth, revised in the light of a later reading, and only so far idealized as the issues attained and the temper portrayed are ideal themselves. But the personal note is enlarged in the process to one fuller and more *universal*. As the development and redemption of a single soul are followed along the lines of the more permanent historic movements, and under the pressure of the manifold forces of modern life, the limits of individual vision must pass in a sense into a panorama of time, and the confessions of a private spirit become the reflection of an age.

The note, again, of the poem is to be essentially *modern*. I say essentially, for much that seems modern, in life and literature, is apt to be an expression or echo of something secondary, superficial, distorted. But to be contemporary in tone and scope with a time as a whole, to divine and perhaps in part to develop, consciously or unconsciously, whatever in its nature has vitality, energy and persistence, is a lawful dream, nay, an imperative ideal for that form of song of which I would be minister. As one who has lived and striven with many of those spirits which seek to baptize, each into the narrowness of its own name, the abounding life of a whole humanity; as one who at last and hardly has found peace and issue, I cannot but believe that our season is ripe for a new and creative fruitfulness; it may be, for a song to glorify and shape its coming.

Complex, shifting and subtle as are the forces and fashions of our life; deep as are its divisions, its core of revelation can no longer be hidden. The spirit of the century which dawned in revolution and dream, to pass under the powers of reaction and revival, has become at its close critical, self-conscious, scientific, historical. Evolution is the sum and motto of its achievement. No doubt the unhistorical negations of the radical temper, and the unhistoric affirmations of the reactionary, are still operant. But they are as much survivals as the merely mechanical methods of undeveloped science. To-day life has become the supreme category; growth the central conception; unity the dominant ideal. Life, growth, unity—these are the faces which the spirit of the age presents to such as question at its oracles, and from these must be read its answer of desolation or comfort. Whether the voice be prophetic of denial or affirmation, its interpretation henceforth can only be historic. To many, indeed, criticism would seem no more than a solvent; self-consciousness a gospel of disease and contradiction; science an unveiling of the nakedness of nature; history a long disproof of its own aspirations. To these life must appear illusion or disillusion; growth an increasing sense of the depths of dualism; and unity only a mocking vision or a violent disendowment. But such mistake a partial and temporary denial for a permanent response, whereby the spirit of a time, which they but half envisage, becomes the burden and echo of their own limitations. But for those who face that spirit with the fullness of insight; who, approaching its presence in its own temper, have tried and sifted its manifold expressions; who have pierced to the heart of its positive meaning; who have learnt that it carries with it its own correction; who can divine the range of its deeper possibilities; who will allow for its growth and wait upon its fulfilment—for such, I say, its oracles at the last are clear and reassuring. For them evolution has the secret and revealing of a new confidence. Taken in its breadth as a method alike of fulfilment and redemption, it rebaptizes the past and preforms the future. In the light and faith of its large historic reason, nature, self and time put on a new glory and hope of growth. Nature has been reconsecrated by science as a fuller and freer shrine of true divinity. Self is seen to have been shattered by criticism, subtilized and saddened by inwardness for a deeper reconciliation. Time has been recovered and vitalized by regressive historical sympathy as a condition and prophecy of fresh development. Indeed to preach and effectualize a more real and deliberate return to nature, self, and history, has been the spiritual work of the century which is ending. The task which now looms upon the energies of the next, is to appropriate from movements, which have often been propagated with excess, partiality, or exclusiveness, their deeper and more positive issues; to transcend the limits of their several revelations, and to fuse and reconcile their results in a living and organic whole. By it will be built a new period of creation on the basis of criticism. By it the depths of inward division, with which the spirit is troubled, will be spanned by another and subtler bridge. By it the sum of science will be hallowed and humanized with a larger and more imaginative sympathy, the vision of nature and law transfused with the light of a diviner prophecy. By it the inheritance of the past will be resumed in a spirit both of expiation and fulfilment. A fresh and fuller unity in life and thought, in society and religion, is ready to grow from the deepened and sifted soil, with a confidence more serene, because its consciousness is scientific and sober. That life will grow effectually to a whole and noble accomplishment in proportion as it finds itself anew, freed, fulfilled and reconciled in God. On us it is laid to recover the Divine, as at once process and perfection, in self, in nature, in time; and to realize again the personal unity which overlooks and rounds our oppositions, with a breadth of consecration superseding all contrast of sacred and secular, and with a fullness of fusion which shall harmonize the whole man in a higher aspiration. Those who have felt most patiently, and with the prophecy of insight, the pulse of our time, know that it is already awaking to light and health. For them the brooding dreams of decadence, exhaustion and denial, which some have welcomed and glorified as a morbid revelation, and others have watched and deplored as the proof of dissolution, are nearing their term.

Whoever believes in the nearness and reality of such a renascence, a renascence broader, more conscious, more conciliatory because it is one and historical, must confess that art and song will find their account in its coming. Perhaps song must wait yet for the full hour, when it shall enter on the inheritance of this fresh inspiration; must wait till it can move under the breath of the new spirit with buoyancy and ease, over waters which are still troubled and turbid from the storms of transition. Yet even for those who have weathered hardly the stress of that period, and have attained with loss and regret to the hope of harbourage, there may be forthcoming a song preparatory, transitional, and, in a measure, prophetic. To me, at least, it has seemed that song may mediate between these ages already blending. Criticism, whether philosophic or literary, can breed, I believe, a music of its own, at any rate as a prelude to more creative harmonies. The broken and overstrung chords of inwardness may be retuned and retouched to the tones of a freer and fuller sanity. The face of nature, now lined with law, may be shown to reveal a young and more spiritual loveliness. The spirit of history may be shapen and transfigured into visual forms for its own fulfilment. It will be said, I know, that a song such as this, by assuming the functions of philosophy and religion, is charging itself with an alien load. Yet song, by inherent law, whether with instinct or deliberation, in virtue of that ideal insight which is at once recovery, prophecy and realization, endeavours to reconcile; and so far must be already in principle and spirit both reasonable and religious. Its specific privilege is to idealize and unify more freely, in modes personal and passionate, melodious and imaginative.

I said above that one note of this poem was to be essentially modern. The drift of my meaning will now be apparent. It is an attempt to embody, even in such personal and imaginative forms, with directness and deliberation, the spirit of our age, in the phases of its denial and in the fullness of its positive promise. One who has lived through those phases, and realized that promise, can read in himself the reflection of their life. To represent such a life, personal and common, as a growth which has reabsorbed a full organic sustenance from the roots of the past, and which has been quickened thereby to push forward a flower of faith and vision into the spring of the future, is the sum of his purpose. What has been sung has been lived, and it has been sung because it has been lived. Whether such a life, which has found its impulses of development and methods of redemption in the manifold paths of criticism and history, of science and self-consciousness, of philosophy and art, of love and religion, can be a fit subject for song, is not my question. But if, in being personal and modern, this poem has become philosophic, religious, historic, remedial, I can only say that such is the quality and intrinsic texture, and such the true aspiration and need of life contemporary.

For a poem and subject thus conceived the title "Two Lives" is not a misnomer. For me it covers a fullness of meaning, some aspects of which I have sought to express

PREFACE. xiii

in a poetical preface. The dualism of life and its growth to unity by many methods and opposing impulses, are the deeper ideal issues which underlie the limited but true and passionate experience of a private soul. From this point of view the unity of the poem may be best envisaged. It has, or would have, that personal unity which belongs to the genuine expression of living experience, represented as a growth with definite limits and a true satisfaction. It has the larger unity which is born of an effort to realize and reflect the spirit of an epoch. It has also the ideal unity which is derived from the pressure of certain central and dominant beliefs, from the insistent thought of a new fulfilment, and from a dream of foreshowing and sharing in its remedial methods.

I have been thus long in apology for my purpose, because much of its promise must lie beyond the present margin of its fragmentary performance. Of the two cantos here published, the first, beginning in the middle, shows how that purpose, latent and repressed, but ripening for expression, and for which other vehicles and forms of vision seemed once more adequate, in the presence and by the power of death took shape and inspiration as song. The second develops the earlier growth of a nature inherently unhistorical and negative through its many phases of unbelief and emptiness. The later cantos will trace its progress where it is gradually touched and fertilized by the more positive and fruitful influences of life and time, and will strive to express the place and power of their several spirits.

The poetical form in which this purpose has been clothed, was adopted upon a distinct conviction of its fitness for the matter. A narrative of growth, whether passing more calmly on the currents of individual and inner life, or with a larger breath through periods of time, may fairly be unfolded in a metre which, like the Spenserian stanza, has a natural openness of movement and a scope for passionate concentration; and which, by lightening the weight of reflection, and forcing upon it a definite and organic melody, can effectually carry its burden and correct its reluctance. On the other hand, the personal factor has found a freer utterance in the lyrics. These have been introduced at intervals more or less regular, and are meant at the same time to break the monotony of a long development, and to mark and accentuate the main stages of the poem. Such a fusion of Epic and Lyric elements is an admission, no doubt, of a mixture of ideals. Yet fusion, in a sense, is the true solution, spiritual and formal, of our present needs. And so long as a fusion be natural, organic and fruitful, life will be content to look no further for growth and originality.

DEDICATION.

OH love, I know not if this song
    Unblest of thee, my spirit's wife,
    And nurtured in a lonely strife
With death, to whom I half belong,
Shall be hereafter heard among
    The things that do inherit life.

But, if it quickened be to brave
    My winter and the world's, and bloom
    With something of a fresh perfume
Before time's sense, thy sweetness gave
The breath that shall embalm and save
    Its nature from decay and doom.

And since my sorrow now hath wove
    With solemn fingers, skilled by death,
    Into a larger lyric wreath
Some scattered buds that earlier strove
To blossom on the lips of love,
    And blend with thy still living breath;

These flowers, unvital yet, but grown
    On my deep suffering's soil and fed
    Where only love and reverence tread,
Whose scent I would for thee were blown
Abroad, to make thee more mine own,
    I lay beside my living dead.

To thee these flowers, although their worth
    Should wither, now, one life too late,
    With benedictions, I, who date
From thee my being's proper birth,
My spirit's children, born of dearth
    And fullness, thus do dedicate.

DEDICATION.

Oh children of her flesh and mine,
    Within whose tissue tireless skill
    On life's long loom is weaving still
Her substance, and doth subtly twine
Our natures to some new design,
    God's art shall work into your will;

Across the broken thread of space
    And time, to you I here bequeath
    These verses, that perchance, beneath
Their fashion, ye may yet retrace
Her beating heart, her sad calm face,
    And hold for me my love's last wreath;

That, when, from her dead hand increased,
    This creeper shall at length have clomb
    The height of our half empty home,
And fronted with its flush the east,
When the free world to you is leased
    By life, and ye afield must roam,

DEDICATION.

While something yet of her shall make
    Soft shelter for your memory's wall,
    And by my nurture cling and fall
About your senses, I may wake,
By song's clear breath, for her sweet sake,
    Your spirits to her spirit's call;

And she, reborn in your young prime,
    Shall flower above the world's dull dust,
    Though autumn winds may warp and rust
The leaves of my far summer's rhyme,
Which, for your spring, I give [~~leave~~] to time,
    A legacy of song in trust.

Oh brothers dead, whose testament
    Hath freed my nonage to be heir
    Of life, and but for whom I were
An empty thing, homeless, unblent,
Who else had missed my soul's ascent,
    Or striven lonely up time's stair,

DEDICATION.

If now my vision's new presage
　Of private spring must surely draw
　A being, loosened from the law
Of immemorial heritage,
To shape and clamber to an age,
　Your seasons only half foresaw;

If I, who face the future's sun,
　For very growth must half forget
　What time my nature's seed was set,
And how my spirit's tissue spun,
With you these lines still link me one,
　And poorly pay my life's dear debt.

Oh brothers living, by whose hope
　Convoyed, my spirit's bark, less frail,
　Less lonely in its space doth sail
One grey sea widening to God's scope,
Now on a new world's sunward slope
　Your spirits with my song I hail.

DEDICATION.

Oh brothers living hopeless, whom
    Doubt's heavy pole doth still incline
    To one deep winter undivine,
If I, who circle from the gloom
By God's slow season, might illume
    Your underworld, which else were mine,

If even I in song might serve
    And touch again to time's control
    The sickness of an age, whose soul
I felt with all my nature's nerve
From its sane issue start and swerve,
    Or free for perfect vision's whole,

If song itself might half unloose
    The law that plucks two lives apart,
    Half bind one broadening nature's heart
I too were less a thing recluse,
By your free brotherhood's full use,
    For whom I hold this human art.

DEDICATION.

Oh God, since life is but a lyre,
    That seeketh to be strung and thrilled
    By Thee; a temple that should build
Itself deep-based to one pure spire,
Whence it might take Thy spirit's fire,
    And pierce Thine infinite, fulfilled;

Since unto Thee my nature's stream,
    Stained in wild ways, from primal mist,
    By Thy deep law idealist,
Must broaden back—by reason, dream,
Loveliness, death and love supreme,
    Through the full channels of Thy Christ;

If I could compass or sustain
    High notes on such a lyre, or lend
    Pure lips of song, whereby should blend
Anew the passion and the pain
And bliss of worlds, where life is twain,
    And in one breath to Thee ascend;

DEDICATION.

If in such temple my quick sense
    Might feel the very waft and wing
    Of inspiration tune its string
To Thy full music; if more tense,
Transfigured through such reverence,
    My soul might listen there and sing;

If even I, in such full time,
    Between Thy worlds might mediate
    Briefly by song, or recreate
Some shadow of Thy thought, or climb
Some stair of prophecy sublime,
    Myself to Thee I consecrate.

INTRODUCTION.

TWO lives—Her life and mine,
That half unconscious grew
Slowly together, till one love did twine
So close and true
Our several souls, that I had all forgot
The primal law
Of this our individual human lot,
When I awoke and saw,
In the dull dawn of sad surmise,
Death's cold and silent finger come to draw
The curtain from my darkened brain,
And briefly write his legend on my empty eyes—
" Love's life is twain."

Two lives—My life and hers,
Which yet shall grow apart,
Mine upward by the purer pulse that stirs
Its hidden heart,
From the deepest fibre of my memory's root,
On to the flower,
And the far prophecy of perfect fruit,
The hope of whose full hour
Doth quicken every secret seed
Of promise in my waiting will with power
To climb and ripen to the sun
Of her transfigured face, till in its light I read,
Love's life is one

Two lives—The old, the new;
That earlier dream of doubt,
Whose wildness as a rank weed overgrew
Within, without,
The troubled years of my untempered youth,
And even wrought
In her bright spirit, travailing for truth,

By sorrow overtaught,
Such shadows as did haunt our feet,
While, from the twilight level of dead thought,
Sunward we clambered up life's slope,
And all fulfilled and free our vision rose to greet
Clear heights of hope.

Two lives—The new, the old,
When blending ages meet
On the great bar, where time has ever rolled,
With restless beat,
Out of the bosom of a boundless change,
And souls are tossed,
Till some upon the sands and shallows strange
Unpiloted are lost,
And some untravelled tremble back
Under the havens of an ancient coast,
Some ocean-bound confront the foam,
Divine the deepening tide, and take the starry track
To a free home.

Two lives—The brief bare cell
    Wherein doth lonely brood
The barren nature that hath heard no spell
    Of brotherhood,
Or love's enlargement; and the broadening space
    Beyond the bar,
Where the free currents lap and interlace,
    And the full human star
  Luminous looks upon the soul,
Which fareth from a dead self insular
  Outward, where open love doth lose
In the true light and motion of one living whole,
    To find and fuse.

    Two lives—The soul's pure peak,
      Whose dawn and sunset fire
Droppeth reproof and dream of power to seek,
      Till it inspire
Deep in our passion's plain the spirit's law,
      And sense of fall,
Lifting a low world to its upward awe,

INTRODUCTION. xxvii

    Brooding, perpetual.
    The petty truth of this clear ridge;
    That broader blue across the rift, whose call
    Doth haunt and spur all footless art
To fling his airy shape and briefly seem to bridge
    Two lives apart.

    Two lives—The gracious growth
    Of sweet seeds, purely set
For consummation, climbing free, unloath,
    From earth's deep debt
Sunward, as quickened by the spirit's wind,
    And love's light faith;
And things misgrown, unchosen, out of kind,
    Begotten at the breath
Of strife, and shapen by its teem
And very travail, rebaptized in death,
    Tears and regret, till nature wild,
By love's deep logic grown, who doubteth to redeem
    Be reconciled.

Two lives—The human woof,
　　The mystic warp divine,
Woven by God, who worketh not aloof
　　To his design
Intrinsic; whither all things climb and cross,
　　Fulfilled, begun,
Through death and beauty, dream and love and loss,
　　So subtly pieced and spun
　　By His pure Spirit, He doth use
The whole world's service, sacramental, one,
　　Unto its form's full continent,
For high prophetic truth, and doth Himself infuse,
　　Till twain be blent.

　　Two lives—whereby we grow,
　　　　Who else were unfulfilled,
Or dead things flawless; in whose light we know;
　　　　Whereon we build
And see all fair shapes; from whose shore we link
　　　　To love and time
The outward spirit's quest, or inly sink

To deeper self; or climb
Blending and broadening ever; whence
We clasp full future, one with simple prime;
Whose ripening touch imperative
Shapeth one nature's whole through human transience
To die and live.

One life to be—more large,
Fuller, more human, free,
If passion's wind sweep not o'er nature's marge;
One mystery,
Method and dawn of vision more divine;
One widening trail
Of truth more common, and one deepening line
Of beauty, whose pure hail
Calleth us to its purple shore,
Whither, one broadening brotherhood, we sail,
Linked subtly back by time's true bond,
Blown on by liberty, blending new nature's lore
With worlds beyond.

CANTO I.
DEATH. NATURE. SONG.

WINTER.

TWO winters wait upon the birth
 Of this untimely child of song,
 Begotten as I moved among
The seasons of a sunless earth.

One with a white prophetic pall
 Lay brooding evermore above
 The private depths of our dear love,
A dream of death perpetual.

What time the fibres of my life
 Were loosened and my soul awoke,
 About me only children spoke,
And only silence whispered "wife."

Between that winter's length and this
 Less bitter, frozen lips of grief
 Were half unsealed by song's relief
Half broken by remembered bliss.

But, as I stood and summed alone
    The seasons of my year's long pain,
    I saw death's shadow fall and stain
Love's vision underneath a throne.

I know not whether love unwed,
    A crown unworn, a life uncrowned,
    More hopeless were, or love that found
All its fulfilment in the dead.

That common garb and heart of woe
    Was royal shroud for crownless king,
    Their grief, I doubt not, was a thing
Less deep for such an overflow.

My sorrow I have told to song,
    God knoweth, in a doubting hope
    That it may win there truer scope,
And make at last my weakness strong.

And so, perchance, my love, unlost,
    Shall pass to some more subtle power
    Of formless heat; my life shall flower
More fruitful for this deadly frost.

And I must deem my nature's nerve
    By death himself was thus restrung,
    That I should be as one who sung
How sorrow learnt from love to serve.

TWO LIVES.

1

Dead, dead! Who is it dreaming here alone,
    Here on the very heart and lap of life,
Dreaming of death? I know not. Were he known
    To me, though inly worn by strain and strife,
    And visited by doubtful visions, rife
With grave regret and longing, he could break,
    At one light whisper of the dear word " wife,"
The bondage of his nature and awake,
To clasp the living world with her, for her sweet sake.

2

Dead, dead! He cannot wake. No whispers come.
    That overbrooding ear is grown too dull
To catch such low and loving utterance. Dumb
    Unto his spirit, which it once would lull
    Or quicken, till it seemed to disannul
All sense of severance, is this fair day, fraught
    With tempered melody and meaning full,
Half promised June, half April unforgot.
He cannot hear alone. Away! I know him not.

3

Only the north-wind, now a whisper, stirs
    The hawthorn blossom, which o'ershadoweth
His sorrow, while he listens but for hers.
    And she is silent. Oh, if her sweet breath
    Blent with the wind and voiceless, as beneath
He dreams, would touch his brow! O God, her kiss,
    Cold though he felt it from the lips of death,
Come back to him! I'd say it was not his;
But mine, mine, mine, and claim such sadness for my bliss.

4

Oh no! Not mine. I am as one aloof,
    Looking on sorrow's face; my being whole,
Or broken but by thought, and passion-proof
    My senses. Surely now some other soul,
    Adept in suffering, hath unbidden stole
Into the secret places of my brain,
    And there, upon its surface, as a scroll,
Writ dimly out, with one dull word's refrain,
The prophecy and burden of an alien pain.

5

Dead! Shall I see it written on the wall
   Of my dark spirit's chamber, as I rise,
In the grey dawn of grief perpetual,
   To pore and ponder with mechanic eyes,
   Watching the weary hours of sad surmise
Live slowly out, and hollow day succeed
   This twilight mood of lingering mysteries,
   Till in full vision and unveiled I read
The secret sense of death, and do accept his creed?

6

What is yon phantom? Oh my sense is sick
   For very emptiness and lack of her.
It brings for sweet fulfilment's food some trick
   Of fancy, as a false interpreter.
   It moves to greet me through the mists that blur
The mirror of my future. On its brow
   Is branded sorrow's seal. Strange lips, that stir
   And speak not, seem to shape, "I leave thee now."
"I wait. Hereafter read my legend, 'This is thou!'"

7

Ay! But there should have been another shape,
    Not faint as this or unfamiliar;
At whose bright rising I had found escape
    From shadows of myself, which haunt and mar
    The glass of my foreshowing. From afar
No motion now comes unto me, no gleam
    Of loyal eyes, for mine have lost their star,
In driving mists of death and tears that stream.
I cannot see beyond. Leave me to-day to dream.

8

Ah me! I dare not dream. I dreamt last night.
    Methought that I was standing at her door,
And saw my sweet within, by the wan light,
    Wearing the simple black that once she wore,
    When, at our first full kiss, we learnt the lore
Of love made perfect. Pale she stood, a stone,
    And cold, as she was never wont before,
And crying "come not" in a troubled tone,
Left me in outer darkness with my love alone.

9

There was a season sweet, when I could climb,
　Above the breathless level of to-day,
To-morrow's height, a libertine of time;
　When my free spirit, swept with hers away,
　In full presage and awe did seem to pray
Uplifted in wide worship; or descend,
　Time-travelled and content, as life grew grey,
To the dim world of dreams, where mine would blend
With hers, or in her warm and breathing presence end.

10

No dream, no dawn visits me here. I dwell,
　If that this sleepless solitary mind
Be very I, within a brief bare cell
　Of everlasting now. Before, behind,
　Sorrow, as one who deeply hath divined
My unsubstantial self, which would be free,
　Fronts my defiance, whilst I feel him bind
With silent hands, at sullen life's decree,
And rivet round my soul a hard reality.

11

Is there no window in the walls of fate
   To draw my nature up, and bid me snatch
Some fragment of the warm world passionate,
     And blend again with it; with strange eyes watch
     Life's long procession, or but hold a patch
Of bright infinity, which should beguile
     My blank and brooding faculties to catch
   And briefly fix one image of her smile?
I will look out and lose myself a little while.

12

The sun hath sucked the breath of budding May,
   And dreams upon the bosom of the down
In loving light. Around low branches sway
     White with the blossoms born beneath the frown
     Of overstaying March. Above the town
Far south and low doth linger on and brood
     One solemn cloud; and westward looms, to crown
   This stolen noon of summer solitude,
Beyond the hollow gorge a soft and ghostly wood.

13

Full odours from the hawthorn bloom distil,
    Sealing all senses but their own, and keep
In outer courts of hearing, as they fill,
    A world of waiting sounds, that slowly creep
    Into my presence; from the quarried steep
The ring of iron faint; the mystic moan
    Of hidden ships, which haunt the river's sleep;
The beat of hooves in hollow monotone;
Anon the cuckoo's note, and chimes of churches blown.

14

The power of spring is on me. Out of sound
    And interwoven sweetness she has wrought
So rich a spell and subtle, it hath bound
    My senses in a trance, though eager thought,
    And the light spirit's motions answer not.
Only across my vision comes and goes
    The face of nature as of one forgot,
The fashion of a loveliness, that knows
No inward soul of meaning deeper than repose.

15

Last year—or was it in a dateless youth?—
   Not so this season o'er me seemed to drift
Like dreamy autumn. Then its deeper truth,
   Touching me to a correspondence swift,
   Did all my inmost force and feeling lift
To airy worlds of free imagining,
   Where insight wrought with sound. Across the rift,
That rends my life, still there are lingering
Echoes of rhymes which felt the spirit of the spring.

SPIRIT OF SPRING.

THERE'S a power at work in the sleeping wood;
　　There's a secret swelling below in the earth;
There's a subtle spirit that seems to brood
　　On the hidden presage of some new birth.

There's a faint warm presence I dimly feel
　　Creep into the pause of the cold, cold east;
There's a strange cool fragrance beginning to steal
　　From the lap of the land, when the showers have ceased.

There's a dreamy promise that purely dwells
　　On the breast of the meadow in purple mist;
There's a soft red flush on the tree, that tells
　　Of myriad buds sun-quickened and kissed.

There's a whisper abroad, and the west wind's breath
　　With a mystic and richer meaning is rife;
There's a waking rumour of winter's death;
　　There's a sigh in his heart for a coming life.

There's a flutter of joy in the bird's free mind,
   There's a formless hope in his fuller song,
From a message he learnt at the lips of the wind,
   From a vision he saw, as the light grew long.

There's an echo awake on the inmost chord
   Of the soul that trembles and tries to sing,
Till into the music of one sweet word
   The sense of thy mystery melts, O spring!

16

Perchance it might have been my spirit's spring,
   And, waste and fallow with six winters' cold,
My frozen faculties, that sought to sing
   But sang not, might have woke and heard foretold
   Fresh hopes of summer song, which should unfold
To fullness; might have seen prevision melt
   Into a free impassioned power to mould
For shapely life and utterance thoughts, that dwelt
Voiceless and void below, and fashion all I felt.

17

But now, O mocking May, thy forward look
　I follow not. To me more welcome March,
Whose bitter mood and scornful surely took
　　The image of my own, and seemed to search
　　An empty world, under one low grey arch,
With hollow sighing. Now for me no shoot
　　Shall overlive the winds of death, which parch
And wither all the future of my fruit,
And bend me back upon the past's undying root.

18

This is a poorer nature than I knew,
　And loved with other eyes. Once she was kind;
And face to face our long communion grew
　　So close and secret, the prophetic wind
　　Breathed not to man her quintessential mind
More truly than to me. Then I could feel
　　The breadth of all her being intertwined
With mine, and in our meeting dear reveal
And consecrate our love with freedom's simple seal.

19

For she had learnt the seasons of my soul,
    Moving within the unimagined room
Of her wide spirit's world; and sometimes stole
    Through golden gates from underneath the gloom,
    That lifted late and seldom to illume
My evening with her light; and from life's flower
    Drew subtly forth a sudden rich perfume,
Holding all sense and passion, thought and power,
Fused in the solemn fullness of one sunset hour.

20

Anon her quickening spirit would unswathe
    An all too speculative vision, dim
With days of listless doubt, and bid me bathe
    In her deep sea of beauty. Eye and limb,
    Made strong and buoyant by her love, would swim
Over her bosom, feel her splendour purge
    All petty life, and, broadening to the rim
Of liberal space, with swift outgoing merge
An importuning self in pure emotion's surge.

21

Yet held she not my nature idly lapt
  In still enchantment, no, nor wholly lost
To individual sense. For I was rapt
  From inward musing, over waters crossed
  By undercurrent sounds, to a high post
Prophetic, whence her light and gleaming wand
  Pointed my motions to a nameless coast,
That led me ever forth by ways unconned,
Infinite and unbroken, of a world beyond.

22

So would I travel out, as one unfraught,
  On exaltation's wave; so wander back
Replenished with her riches, until thought,
  Waiting for ever in emotion's track,
  Awoke, and, as it felt the current slack
Of outward faring life and vision, pressed
  Into the pause, to gather of the wrack,
And treasure up its fullness for my rest,
Then quicken once again free feeling on her quest.

23

O large and open unto me her love,
  Whose free essential wind and common air,
Sweeping around me, for awhile unwove
  Time's texture from my life, and raised it bare
  To ecstasy; or if I wandered there
Breathless as in a void, she drew me down,
  To blend with all her loveliness, and wear
And win this law of beauty for my own,
"Fulfilment maketh free, and calm is passion's crown."

24

O close and dear our meeting. Yet aloof
  Her spirit moved. From some far central shrine
Of privacy, she touched with pure reproof
  My passion; and I learnt the subtle sign,
  Wherewith she slowly schooled me to divine,
Under the show and vesture of her change,
  A viewless presence, rounding hers and mine,
And left me trembling on a threshold strange,
Still unfulfilled in her sweet revelation's range.

25

I gazed again, and found free nature's face
 Transfigured, as of one that dared to climb
And lift my longing over bars of space
 To a world specular of life sublime,
 Invisible.   I felt her motions rhyme
With the long march of everlasting law;
 And fresh and full the purpose of her prime
Looked forth upon me, till it seemed to draw
My sight and spirit out into impassioned awe.

26

They say that nature showeth in a glass
 To man, her offspring and a visitant
At her dim oracle, in shapes that pass,
 Only a shadow of himself; that want
 Is to his eye a false hierophant,
Mocking with misconception; that we find
 Such images of comfort as we plant
Her ground withal; that fancy, sowing blind,
Reaps for her sustenance an unsubstantial wind.

27

Not so her meaning took me.   Deep and clear
   Out of her sanctuary an answer stole
Upon my emptiness.   And I could hear,
   Around the quiet island of my soul,
   That ocean world of hers harmonious roll.
I was an echo only, and I caught
   From the full glory of her spherèd whole
Only a gleam, as, under sound and thought,
I clasped a kindred life sublimer than I sought.

28

Ay, and her spirit looked beyond her speech,
   Though full the utterance; and its truth outran
Her pale of vision (as high prophets teach,
   Shaping a wisdom wider than the span
   Of private inspiration), broke the ban
Of self and circumstance, and overflowed
   All barriers, broadening ever to the plan
   Majestical of beauty's last abode, [of God.
Where wrought and moved the presence and the power

29

Such fellowship was mine with nature's heart,
   Such privilege. But oh, there came a breath,
The keenness of whose edge had power to part
   Our ancient bond, and blew a hollow wreath
   Of formless mist out of the depths of death,
Which blurred the fair perfection of her face
   With shadows of estrangement. Still beneath,
Though it be overblown, I may not trace
The passion and the prime of unforgotten grace.

30

There is no spot within that ample field,
   Whence death has not withdrawn some primal dower
Of loveliness; no hue that hath not sealed
   Half of its revelation up; no hour
   Of all her seasons but has felt the power
Of strange infection; not a shape but loses
   Some share of proper sweetness; not a flower
From all the company of June but closes
Her golden heart of meaning with the wild, wild roses.

SUMMER.

O THE roses wild!
    Do they grow
Still in that dim green mysterious lane?
    Climbing as they clomb
    On the high hedge overhead,
    Climbing where I once did roam
    Long ago,
Like an all unvisionary child
Seeing, though I saw not, what would mine remain?
    I can never know.
    Let them be disrooted, dead;
    They have found a home
In my heart, and there deep-domiciled,
    And for ever fed
By my love, shall live and blossom in my brain.
    O the roses wild!

    O the roses wild!
    White and red,
Faint as dying lips and fresh as foam,
    On the verge they blow,
    Where the mirrored cliffs do stain

Crimson all the flood below.
    O the dread!
Last year was it briefly once beguiled?
Dread of deathly clouds that seemed to creep and come,
    Closing overhead,
        While for her I gathered twain,
        By the river running low,
    For my love, who looked at me and smiled?
        But the blurring rain
Down upon my heaven drew and swept across my home.
    O the roses wild!

    O the roses wild!
        And the rain!
Children, hers and mine, around me grow,
    But my rose is dead,
    And they gather, as they roam,
        Roses white and red.
            O the pain,
Mocking time that maketh all things mild,
With its thorn will pierce my empty spirit through,
        Till I see again,
    If, within my hollow home,
        Looking overhead
    Love with death be reconciled,
        See the roses blow,
Under benedictions of God's open dome.
        O the roses wild!

31

Speak to me, silent wind! Oh, wherefore haste,
    Alienate and inscrutable? How long
Shall my heart listening only hear thee waste
    The secret mission of thy lips among
    The wild pines in low privacy of song?
Speak to me, for me, wind! Hast thou not heard?
    I am alone. Oh, be to me a tongue,
From death to life, for all that ever stirred
Of love or longing there, and bless me with a word.

32

Wilt thou not wait for me, oh careless cloud,
    Winged prophet of the pure and free north-west,
That I may wander forth with thee, endowed
    With the swift joy of motion, on thy quest,
    And win beside thee, as thou visitest
All farthest forms, prevision clear? Oh, sweep
    Me from my memory loose, or let me rest
By thy light shadows as they pass and creep
From field to field, or linger where the low woods sleep.

33

Oh, red is still the heather, where we stood,
  Only one August—and a life—ago,
And felt it flushing to our hearts. There's blood
  Upon the blossom now. It could not grow,
  Had not the grudging winds, that never blow
One seed of consolation into ken
  Of my dull sense of craving, come to sow
  Abroad the message of my sorrow. Then
It should have withered back to barren grey again!

34

Red is the heather by the ring of firs,
  That overpeering, dark and dominant,
Our purple ridge, can watch the sloping spurs
  Creep out amid the corn. Their figures gaunt
  Look giant-like upon the sun, but slant
Their grey and seamèd foreheads from the frown
  Of the besieging west, whose visits haunt
  Their posted pride, and dim, beyond the brown
And broken moorland, see the dreaming southern down.

35

Oh, my thoughts travel out along that fringe
    Of floating blue. It wins me westward, till,
Blent with the mist below, it takes the tinge
    And fashion of a cloud. They follow still,
    Where, far and low within the folded hill,
One readeth words, whose magic seems to move
    By sweet life's promise and prophetic thrill
His spirit, with the sun and sea inwove,
To feel their simple sense, "She loves me and I love."

36

Back to me from behind the clearer south
    The vision comes, more bitter and more sweet,
Of one that moveth to a trembling mouth
    And heart, which cannot stay to breathe and beat,
    And tender eyes, that wait not now to meet
In such full moment all the hope of his
    With consummation's light, growing complete
Together, until all that was or is
Of sunshine gathered there in one untroubled kiss.

37

Oh, life and sunshine ! Could my vision cope
  With faintness, and my fancy turn true seer,
East, in the hollow of that far grey slope,
  Whose forehead breaketh seaward, white and sheer,
  Two souls make love's last covenant. Oh hear,
Ye heavens, and listen earth ! Low words are said,
  Sealing that sweet communion, new, more near,
Which loosens ancient links; and twain are wed,
And welded to one life and love—and she is dead !

38

Oh love, oh life behold me ! She was mine.
  Come back to me ! Oh fix me there amid
The homes and hollows of that distant line,
  My soul's horizon ! Hold my being hid
  In those three years, whose sweet worth shall outbid
Time's competition ! Let their briefness last,
  Immortal and aloof, for ever rid
Of hopeless memory's phantom word, "thou wast,"
Under the purple light, which lingers on the past.

39

Oh death, dull realist, wouldst thou abridge
    Such blessing? Wouldst thou free me from all taint
Of dream and vision, that from ridge to ridge
    Thou hast recalled me by thy cold restraint,
    Slurring the land, that lies unpictured, faint,
Like to my after life, back to this knoll,
    Where thou shalt show me to myself, and paint
Into the eye and centre of the whole,
Deep-shadowed on the past my solitary soul?

40

Oh nature, hast thou dowered me with thy gift
    Of free enlargement only to this end,
That I may watch with thee and see the rift
    Widen upon my life, and only spend
    Thy riches on my emptiness? False friend,
Thou hast conspired with death himself to borrow
    From me my love and yesterday, to lend
Nought to me but the image of my sorrow,
Which closes in to-day and overclouds to-morrow.

41

Oh love, oh wife, oh friend, thy death has bound,
    For my dull scrutiny, and sealed the book
Of nature's benediction. She that crowned
    With loveliness our ways, when I forsook
    Her love for thine, and thy dear power shook
Her sleeping prophecies to life, and smote
    Human and full upon me, mocks my look
Of longing, answering not to my sad note,
But moves mechanic by in law's unlovely rote.

42

Ye cold and quiet witnesses of death,
    Were it not that your beauty still embalms
Deep in its heart a fragment and a breath
    Of her true sweetness; that my empty palms
    Would catch and close upon the meagre alms
Of merest consolation, I could hate
    Your pitiless core of power, which, though it calms
My thought and passion, dared to desecrate
The pale of her dear life, and clasp her in dull fate.

43

Nay, lawless rather, jarred and out of joint
    Seems to me nature's system.   Doubt has torn
The mask from off her fairness, and doth point
    The lean and ghostly finger of his scorn
    Full at her forehead, where she once had worn
The pageantry of life, and doth proclaim
    Her hollow purpose, as of one forsworn,
And showeth in a bare unreverend frame
Death's own deep-riven flaw, the secret of her shame.

44

Ay—She has nothing in me now.   And yet,
    Strange stealthy ministrations will intrude
On empty hours, when I would fain forget
    Myself; and slowly will unlock my mood,
    With quiet keys of memory, where I brood
Full face with sorrow; ay, and half engross
    The inward eye from sacred solitude,
And wait around my steps, and climb across
All my disrooted life and overgrow my loss.

45

Let them go by! For how should I decline
    On such low comfort, calm although it were?
I who had wholly made a woman mine,
    And climbed her height of love, and lingered there,
    Seeing in nature but a broken stair
Of aspiration, whence my soul should win
    A larger insight, over fields more fair,
Into the sweetness of a heart akin,
And all the secret places of the world within.

46

Or is there healing in the empty hand
    Of death? and did I all too lightly dream
That nature's face would meet mine, ever bland?
    And if with all my sadness she could seem
    Sad, yet my heart divined not half the scheme
Of the mysterious love behind her smile
    And tears, to raise hereafter and redeem
Out of the depths, where I must dwell awhile,
Till I confess and prove her power to reconcile?

47

Doubtless to her at last I shall return,
    In my full season, and her period
Of secular renewal; shall discern,
    But with a vision freer and more broad,
    And purged in ways of womanhood and God,
How life and death by her low hidden path
    Divinely blend in some sublimer road,
And, reaping what I may of aftermath,
Regather all she gave and deepen all she hath.

48

And doubtless she will come divinely back
    For my refreshment, and will slowly wean
My feet from following only on the track
    Of grudging death, where I may hardly glean
    One ear, which to my sorrow shows not lean
And blighted, till she crown a far belief
    With God's grain, subtly moulded out between
Death's chemistry and life's, and for my grief
Bring ripe into my heart a full and golden sheaf.

AUTUMN.

AUTUMN held me as my soul's own season,
    When my fancy freshly moved along
Time's procession. Yet I meant no treason
    To proud summer's place, no wrong
    Unto tender spring, or winter pure and strong.
Love was all my reason,
    And the year was ripe for song.

Fairest was the face of soft October,
    In the golden days, when she was kissed
By the sun of June, but joy was sober,
    Mellowed in a dream of mist,
    Joy of sweet transition, unto her that wist
Cold winds would unrobe her
    For true winter, keeping tryst.

Oh, but this year's faith was early broken ;
    Every hope was hollow ; not a breath
Of true autumn took me ; all unspoken,

TWO LIVES.

    Dropped her secret into death,
    Leaving, of the beauty buried underneath,
On the earth, in token,
    But a soiled and sodden wreath.

Out of all the ample heart of nature,
    Once so human, to my soul confined
Here amid the ways of men, in stature
    Dwarfed and shrunken, songless, blind,
    No life cometh now, or dieth undivined,
Nothing but misfeature,
    Falling leaf and barren wind.

Lonely, silent, there is one that paces,
    Autumn overhead and at his feet,
Lost in some far season, where he traces,
    Moving on from street to street,
    Two ways, where the whole world once for him could meet,
Seeing but two faces,
    Hearing but two hearts that beat.

Homeward, homeless, early, late, he goeth,
    Where the gaunt and gnarled acacias loom
Leafless, where the cold laburnum showeth
    Withered phantoms of her bloom,
    Where the lilac shed her sweet life's faint perfume,

TWO LIVES.

Where the white birch boweth
  Ghostly in the autumn gloom.

Only at the window of a chamber,
  Is it mine? where love doth wake and call,
Autumn leaves are flushing still from amber
  Into crimson. Let them fall!
  Let them cling and wither, or upon the wall
Peer awhile and clamber!
  Autumn, all is over, all.

Gold.—But yesterday the world was golden.
  Golden was the month our spirits met,
When, beneath time's soft wings briefly folden,
  Lips were trembling to forget
  In fulfilment's hour far longing's gathered debt.
Would that hour were holden,
  Perfect in its passion, yet.

Brown is all the gold; and now November,
  Brooding on the silent year unseen,
Dulls with his dank breath life's last red ember,
  Or, with frosty finger lean,
  Plucks a meagre remnant of the host of green.
Year, wilt thou remember,
  Fruit and fulness once have been?

Fruit and fulness, autumn, all is over.
　　Life, and I have gathered what thou hast.
Mist and sunshine; I was once a lover;
　　Let me grow upon my past!
　　Let me see thee, love, by some divine forecast,
Climb again and cover
　　My unsheltered home at last!

49

Death came and dwelt with me. I looked without,
　　And thought, although I hardly seemed to think,
That nature, who had soothed an earlier doubt,
　　Could soften truth. I stood beside the brink
　　Of her sweet waters, and I longed to drink
Out of her cup of comfort, to peruse
　　The pure reflection of her love, or sink
Under life's surface for awhile, and lose
Myself in ministrations she might not refuse.

50

For I had loved and waited on her first,
   With loyal service of the soul and eye;
Nor looked not in my hour of lonely thirst
   That she, my spirit's mistress, would belie
   The bounty of her love, or meet me dry
And withered in life's drought. And lo! among
   The empty wells of her mirage, and by
The wilderness of death, she cooled my tongue,
Bidding my powers swell and blossom into song.

51

So deep her skill, so subtly had she dealt
   With me and sorrow, that her very dearth
Of vision turned to sound. And, whilst I felt
   The dead face of an unfamiliar earth
   Decline to nothingness from dearest worth,
Under my straining ears I heard a string
   Vibrating with the pangs of nobler birth,
And knew myself re-born by suffering,
Half found and half forgot, as one who strove to sing.

52

Surely there lives in nature's hand a touch
    Deeper and more divine than any chord,
Whose echoes only ring in hearts of such
    As suffer not, nor know the overlord
    Of love and life—true pain.   For through the word
Of finest resonance it trembles till
    It pierce the secret seat, where lieth stored
The potency of elemental will,
And life is loosened by the deep dissolving thrill.

53

Thus was she gracious to me.   But indeed
    I deem not that the boon was wholly hers,
But rather ripe fruition from a seed
    Dropped on her lap by death, who ministers
    To love, and by his very keenness spurs
And stings imagination to o'erleap
    A low world's seeming, as his wild breath stirs
Fair life's unrippled face with wholesome sweep,
And shakes the heart where love has never learnt to weep.

54

Oh strange that, in the season of her prime,
 All the ripe fulness of her breath would rush
Over my open bosom; yet no rhyme
 Returned the challenge, which could only flush
 The fancy. Then mere sweetness seemed to crush
O'erladen sense. And now, though winter strip
 Her grace and numb her motions, till they brush
But faintly my dull face, she bids me dip
Into deep thoughts that rise and tremble to the lip.

55

More strange that she, the woman who was queen
 Of my poor world, unpeopled of all bliss
But her, who rose and briefly shone between
 One starless night which knew her not, and this,
 Whence she is fallen out, by dearest kiss
That purified my lips, never awoke
 A word within them, but it seemed to miss
The authentic meaning of my love, and broke
The whole harmonious sound I heard but left unspoke.

56

O God! If thou wouldst give me back my dead
    One briefest moment, that, although my breath
Were scant and laboured, as when her dear head
    Dwelt on my bosom by the banks of death,
    For loving ears I might at last unsheath
My heart of all the shame, wherewith I strove
    Voiceless in vain, or lay this lyric wreath,
Which withers even as I write, above   [move.
Her pale pure brow, and mark those faithful faint eyes

57

I do remember—love has writ the date
    Over the ruined entrance of my life—
Before I dreamed that she would dedicate
    Her pureness to my power, and whisper "wife"
    To my most secret self; when laughing strife
Of light words still betrayed not we were stealing,
    Spirit to spirit nearer, mine o'er-rife
With all the labour of vain love's concealing,
And hers unruffled yet by coming love's forefeeling;

58

I do remember how a phantom hope
  Of formless song, which ever came to haunt
My sleeping spirit, caught a clearer scope
  Of purpose, hovering as a visitant
  In the lone world of love's impassioned want,
Wherein I sojourned, beckoning me to build
  Myself into such music, she should grant
An ear of graciousness, and briefly stilled
Doubting desire, then fled hollow and unfulfilled.

59

And after, when so sweetly she came down
  From her far heaven unsphered, and deigned to dwell
Amid my twilight, fair fulfilment's crown
  Lay on my life. Her quiet eyes would quell
  The unrest and fever of my own, and fell
With new enchantment on my sense, and wove
  About my weakness and my strength a spell,
Whose subtle music overwhelmed and drove
My dream of song aloof by countercharm of love.

60

Love was enough; and love alone was near.
    And that no alien voice or hour might thwart
His own pure prophecy, which twain might hear,
    He drew my silent soul with hers apart,
    Where touched and tunable by nature's art
Divinely human, needing not a tongue,
    All the tumultuous meaning of his heart,
Trembling as ours, beat softly out among
The secret chords of life, which love himself had strung.

61

Love was enough, love only. For he breathed,
    Out of the precincts of his power and grace,
A full mysterious spirit forth, and wreathed
    My being in essential life's embrace,
    And closed my vision, whilst before my face
His benediction seemed to pass and steal
    All limits from my soul, but the last space
Of individual fate; then laid a seal
Of silence on my lips, till I had learnt to feel.

62

Love was enough. Upon my lonely earth
  Looked down from all the night a single star.
But it was mine, born with my nature's birth,
  And orbing on me, dear, familiar,
    Over the low grey clouds that rose to bar
From its free scope and need of skyward range
  A darkened vision, though she felt afar
The shadow of eclipse, by prescience strange,
Showed ever one fair face to all my spirit's change.

63

Oh it was plotted in the mind of fate,
  Nature's astrologer, and known to God,
That the twin star of song should rise too late
  For her discerning. Then alone love rode
  And ruled my heaven for a period,
Unsung, unpublished; so that her true height,
  Sinking upon my sense, should find abode
In silent worship through my waiting night,
And draw my broken thoughts to her pure spirit's light;

64

That life might round and polish the dull glass
    Of my rough faculties with edge of pain,
Till the pure radiance of love's beam could pass,
    Unbroken and unblurred by any stain
    Of self or sense; and that, in full refrain,
The essential music of his sphere should rhyme
    With all the courses of my restless brain,
A sound so large and living it should climb
Up to the ears of death, and tremble into time.

65

So love was with me, in a soul unripe
    For his full presence, till free passion stirred
New secret seeds to clamber to the type
    And stature of himself; and, as a bird,
    Wandered from some far shore, with tones half heard,
Haunted my summer, a sweet antidote
    To doubt and solitude, but lent no word,
    Or but a poor and fragmentary note,
To lift a wingless thought, and ease a troubled throat.

66

Yet song lay waiting for his perfect season,
    Deep-folded in my dreaming nature's core;
And peeping out for spring, when winds of reason
    Had swept the thought of all the world before
    My loosened spirit, and had made the lore
Of labour mine, deemed that at last below
    The surface of my soul, through every pore
Of life, would pierce the sun of love and glow,
And push a blossom forth and be its power to grow.

67

But it was winter still, and the dim shape
    Of death loomed out of time, and stood above
The fragment of our life, seeming to drape
    In white mist all the meaning of our love,
    When for her hearing, though the words did move
In their high function, halting, low and weak,
    Half in despair half prophecy I strove
To clasp afar song's pure untravelled peak,
And from its splendour win a path and power to speak.

SONG'S DREAM.

I WOULD that I might feel
    One perfect hour,
When love's own passion-flower
Would blossom in my heart and briefly steal
    My nature; or with solemn power
    A vesper-chime would peal
Of reverence on my mood, and bid me kneel,
Drawing all sense and vision up to their free tower,
    So to unseal,
And show me flushed with awe and beauty's dower
    The whole world and embower
    My spirit there, and heal.
    I would that I might feel
        One perfect hour.

    I would that I might think
        One perfect thought,
      So deep it should be sought
Through summer centuries for men to drink,
      And dry not; so full fraught
       With truth too rare to sink

TWO LIVES.

Under the tide that beats around time's brink;
So purely firm, so rounded and so finely wrought
    Into a link
Within the golden chain of knowledge caught,
    That life could loosen not
    Its clasp, nor fashion shrink;
    I would that I might think
      One perfect thought.

    I would that I might do
      One perfect deed,
    Whose deep root, wholly freed
From the low soil of self and passion, drew
    Its nurture from high human need,
    And, ripening to renew,
Dropped, in the fulness of a time o'erdue,
Into the lap of years a pure and vital seed,
    Which, piercing through
Dead custom, flowered in a simple creed,
    Dying itself to breed
    A broader life as true;
    I would that I might do
      One perfect deed.

    I would that I might find
      One perfect word,
    Whose mirror took unblurred
The very soul of vision and the mind

Of melody; and registered
  The whispering spirit's wind,
And lightest print which fancy left behind;
So quick, that if deep down some strange emotion stirred,
    Dumb, undefined,
Or phantom of dead feeling, half interred,
  Rose in a void, it heard
  A voice, a shape divined;
  I would that I might find
  A perfect word.

  I would that I might sing
    One perfect rhyme,
  Whose ordered march might climb,
Calm as the proud procession of the spring,
  And sweet and light as dewy prime,
    Unbroken but to bring
  The marshalled steps of its free following
By pleasant pause to solemn heights of sound sublime,
    Where, listening
Unto the music of its full true chime,
    The trembling heart of time
    Might beat and swell and ring;
    I would that I might sing
      One perfect rhyme.

    I would that I might make
      One perfect song,

So flawless, that among
The canonizèd few it still should take
The careful eye of praise; so strong,
No breath of age should shake
The blossoms of its honour down, or break;
So surely touched and true to the one human tongue,
It should awake
The drowsy ear of memory to prolong
Its echoes old and young,
For its own simple sake;
I would that I might make
One perfect song.

68

So on life's surface, listening to a dream
  Of distant south, lay my light bark too long,
Becalmed, or floating aimless on a stream
  Of thoughts unshapen, motionless among
    The images that rose and fell. But song
Lingered, until there came a sudden wind,
  Keen with the bitterness of death and strong
To shake my drooping sails, and swept my mind
Shoreward at last by ways deeper than I divined.

E

69

Life unto death.—There is no kingdom, creed,
    No flower or human soul, no vital root
Of thought and aspiration, that can breed
    Right offspring of itself, or freely shoot
    To its full stature, or behold the fruit
Of far perfection in the life of time,
    Or on the lips of men, but death transmute
Decay and weakness into power to climb,
And purge the earth which clogged and overlay its prime.

70

Death unto life.—When all the world is worn
    Beneath the burden of its years, and dearth
Dwells with the present, whose few flowers are born
    Blighted, and life lies fallow, through the earth,
    Out of the depths of some pure past, whose worth
Was drained not, runs a thrill which hath beguiled
    Her heart from barrenness, and in the birth
Of the strange future's fair prophetic child
The great twin powers of time are blent and reconciled.

TWO LIVES.

71

Death unto life.—Oh doubtless it was law,
   With signature and seal of God, deep writ
High on time's forehead. There it seemed to draw
   Life's dreamful fragments to one vision, lit
   With truth's own lightning. There it showed me knit
The great world's seasons secular, that roll
   From spring to spring, recurrent, infinite,
And linked in one harmonious living whole
With all the petty periods of the several soul.

72

Oh doubtless it was law—impersonal,
   Luminous, common, passionless, aloof,
Like some cold star. Ay, but to see it fall
   One private flash on me; to watch the proof
   Break sheer upon my sight down from the roof
Of the world's reason; and to feel it turn
   To fiery potency within the woof
And tissue of my life, that I might learn
In the fierce school of pain how purest truth can burn!

73

Death unto life.—Had that death been but mine,
  Not hers, with all my faculties unblown,
Unripened, touching there true anodyne
    For imperfection, I had passed alone
    Out of this twilight world of love and moan,
Content if only her dear hand had pressed
    Mine, had her sweet tears shriven me, her tone
Of benediction calmed me on my quest,
And I had ceased to breathe only upon her breast.

74

Ay, but to live, where love itself was warm;
  To breathe, to dream, where love itself lay dead;
To wake and fold within a hollow arm
    Only chill memories; to softly tread,
    Trembling as in a world untenanted;
To listen and to hear nought but the knell
    Of dear love's daily parting; to be wed
Body and soul to one live pain; to dwell
Familiar with death's face alone—how were that well?

75

To overlive love's autumn, and to save
  Hardly from his last season one bare seed
To grow withal; and on love's very grave,
  Feeling new fibres tremble to the need
  Of light and motion, there perforce to feed
On the deep memories which rise and mould
  The shape and seeming of a flower, but breed
Nor sap nor sweetness, and to watch unfold
Only a pallid life, like that first primrose cold,

76

Which blossomed over her; ay, and to haunt
  Daily the threshold of death's barrèd hall;
To hold poor piteous hands that close on want,
  Or ineffectual beat against a wall
  Blank and impalpable; oh God, to call
Softly in love's deep silence, and to strain
  All faculty and passion to forestall
The faintest whisper, wafted back again
Into the spirit's pause and broken ebb of pain—

77

How were that well? And how, if life be mute,
    Might I consent to listen unto death,
And watch those pale lips of love's substitute,
    Shaping an answer, as of one that saith—
"I am thine inspiration; my cold breath,
More kind than love, shall quicken thee and bring
    To birth full music, while it uttereth
A note, to whose pure function thou must string
Thy broken nature now, and school dead love to sing."

78

"Dead love shall lend thee sound and vision; so
    Hereafter thou shalt read true prophecy
Perchance in her hard saying."—"Love, I go;
    Forgetfulness, fulfilment, God are nigh;
    And if I seem too human still to die,
Such little fingers hold me here, possessed
    Of dear life's longing, not for thee I sigh,
Knowing thy life shall fare, by this bequest,
Better henceforth alone, for thou hast loved my best."

79

Dear love, dead wife, or if there be a name
   Sweeter than these, more sacred, though my tongue,
Poor silent heretic, felt a quick flame
   Of protestation leap against the wrong,
   Done by thy doubting love to mine less strong,
And lightly would renounce, were I their lord,
   The whole world's legacy and hope of song,
And what is most immortal, for one word
Fresh from thy lips to chime with my life's tuneless chord,

80

Strengthen me, that my passion may not chafe,
   Solely insurgent on usurping death,
Or weakly bend and sue that he vouchsafe
   Some vision to my sense; nor wear a wreath
   Of barren silence; help me here, beneath
His eye, to arm my sorrow and accept,
   For my fulfilment, what thou wouldst bequeath
Of life made fruitful by the tears I wept,
And waken by quick pain my secret powers that slept!

81

Pardon me that I see the hollow wraith
    Of music, which would haunt and half deceive
My dreaming, turning now to solid faith
    Of shapely song; pardon, if on this eve
    Of death, when I perchance might better leave
Love's sanctity true-templed here alone,
    Spiritual, formless in my soul, I weave
Its inmost meaning into words, whose tone
Shall meet the common air and blend me with my own.

82

Oh not with will untuned to thine, dear wife,
    Or lips by thine unpurified I take
From my most private heart thy hidden life,
    And here with trembling hands and reverent break
    Death's heavy seal, not tearless now; nor make
Confession to the public priest, true art,
    Only for human absolution's sake,
Or lightly seeking to discharge my heart
Of sorrow's solemn debt, which I must pay apart.

83

If I were silent then, oh love, forgive,
    When life's full function rose and would repress
My song; if now I sing, who hardly live
    Without thee, deem not that I love thee less,
    Since, into this my world of emptiness,
Thy dear dead image cometh to incite
    My mutinous dull powers, and dispossess,
    By viewless transmutation of love's might,
My spirit of myself, to be song's proselyte.

84

Dead love—not dead, it hath no sweetness thus;
    Oh living love, albeit never song
Fell from thy lips, so true and tremulous
    To the world's beauty mirrored clear among
    Thy visions pure; and I but seemed to long,
Uncentred, ineffectual to set free
    From my thought's burden this too pregnant tongue,
    And, unprophetic, shaped its power to be
Master at length amid the lords of melody;

85

Be to me now a presence and a fire,
   Like that frail spirit, song's essential bloom,
A growth too fevered, born but to aspire,
   Wed to the stem of his strong life, to whom,
   Deep-travelled but unstained in doubtful gloom,
The world was sunny as in Asolo,
   Whose wholesome subtle thought once could assume
For thee the office my love must forego,   [flow.
And whet faith's languid edge and clear life's troubled

86

Be to me sanctuary and song! Be mine,
   O living love, that my love may not miss
Full consummation, as the Florentine
   Austere grew perfect for his Beatrice!
   Beckon me to thee! By that last cold kiss
Of consecration hold me, pure as she,
   But warm with magic of remembered bliss!
The love that was keep thou, and quicken me,
For the true power and stature of the love to be!

87

Compass me with clear hope and memory! Touch
   To pure effectual passion all my sense,
Sublimed, transfigured to an utterance such
   As listens unto love in audience
Of death! And if high reason, reverence,
Faith, freedom, love speak at my spirit's birth
   In music grave, wafted I know not whence,
Oh love, dead, living, clothe it in my dearth
Or fulness with thyself and make it something worth!

LOVE AND SONG.

Love.

COME not, oh song, between
    My love and me!
For though thy presence screen
My private soul and thought from scrutiny
    Of sorrow, I would see
Only his haunting face, who hath so truly seen
    My love and me.

Song.

Say not that I conceal!
    When sorrow dies
To song he doth reveal
His perfect vision, and in song's pure eyes
    Mirrors his mysteries;
And, living, from these lips, where love hath set his seal,
    He prophesies.

TWO LIVES.

Love.

Speak not to me, oh song,
   Who wholly gave
  My ear to wait among
Life's fragments, if from silence I might save,
   Were it a single wave,
Of her sweet music ceased, and listen here, how long?
   By love's own grave!

Song.

  Hear me, for I have heard
   Thy love's true tone!
  When it grew faint and stirred
Hardly one heart, it trembled to my own;
   And now, by my breath blown
Softly about thy senses, waiteth for thy word,
   A song unknown.

Love.

  Ask not, oh song, my heart!
   Dead love is there,
  Sacred, enshrined, apart.
Let me go by! For wherefore wouldst thou share
   A soul, unsheltered, bare?
Touch not my lips with thine! Too passionate thou art,
   Too full, too fair.

Song.
Tell me thy love! I need
No other thing.
Say me thy sorrow's creed!
Lend me thy lips, to shape thy suffering!
For song can grow and cling
Unto love's empty home, or on his fulness feed.
Love thou and sing!

88

But what am I that I should deem me ripe
   For this high dedication, or akin
To canonizèd saints of song? My pipe,
   I fear it, yet will mock me, flawed within,
   On lips unprivileged, by music thin
And miscreated; if strong love not give
   Power and precedent, whence I may win
Such elemental sound, full, nutritive,
As shall sustain proud purpose thus to sing and live.

89

There was a day they told me song was dead,
  Or dying for that all his power was faint
With strange infection, which had inly fed
    And stolen on his weakness; a dull taint
    Of doubt o'ersubtle, knowing not restraint
Or passion; until that fine spirit, rife
    With sick and pallid fancies, learned to paint,
  From the dim places of divided life,
The wholesome world in hues of his sad nature's strife;

90

Or like a lawless star, extravagant,
  Spurning the simple period sublime
Of serene passion, ever seemed to pant
    Inordinate for some fierce power to climb
    A void and viewless heaven, whose heart should
With ecstasy; or fallen from true height,
    And lost to the free motion of his prime,
  Circled the large suns living on our sight
With dead mechanic fire, a shrunken satellite.

91

They told me fancy, moving once a maiden
    Through the free fields of loveliness and awe,
A fresh note rising sweet from lips unladen,
    Was grown to womanhood, and felt the flaw
    Of life in strange transition, where she saw,
For surfeit of near knowledge, that first gleam
    Prophetic pass in the cold light of law,
Then stood, all her high faculty of dream
Forgotten, thirsty, silent by song's empty stream.

92

Or if she sang, it was a troubled strain,
    Touched with a broken longing to recall
The far-off passion and the free refrain
    Of simple days; or knowing not her fall,
    Would blindly lift to song's high pedestal
An image of her lowness, and would drape
    The unpurged and petty individual
In the fair seeming of large art, and ape
That pure faith's worship with her lean and languid shape.

93

And I misdoubting heard. For I had felt
  That self-same shadow coldly fall, and creep
Across my being; seen its darkness melt
  Into the substance of my soul, to keep
  A dim court there; not as from clouds that sweep
The forehead of the sea, and lightly slur
  Its pure reflection; but a stain more deep,
Imperious, inward, such as wild winds stir
Over the ocean's heart, and all the heavens blur.

94

Yet even as I doubted, there arose
  A vision and a shape, which stood aloof,
Majestic. On its brow was high repose
  Seated with passion. From clear eyes reproof
  Like reverend stars, haunting the full world's roof,
Looked forth upon me, shaming me to sing,
  While life's whole music woven in the woof
Of that rich utterance seemed to meet and ring
With song itself or love or some diviner thing.

95

"Were song dead, then thou mightest sing his dirge
 In sound so piteous, death should half forget
His proud cold purpose, and behold emerge,
 Out of the very tomb of dear regret,
 A vision only won by pure eyes wet
With love's own insight; mightest carve a stone
 So shapen by free faith with memory met,
That image should reclaim the authentic tone
And spirit of dead song, to echo to thine own.

96

"Were song a-dying; were that pure full flood
 So shrunk and fallen from the wholesome brim
Of life's true level, that it seemed to brood
 Aimless amid the broken banks, which rim
 And prison its low ripple, now too dim
To take the trembling image of one star,
 Yet might a whisper of the sea's large hymn
By recreative faith be caught afar
From the free waves which beat and gather on the bar.

97

"Song is not dead. He sleepeth; and the dawn,
　Pure flushing for prophetic eyes, which make
To-morrow, were but doubt's cold curtain drawn
　From the free vision, now should surely break
　The seal at last of his dull dreaming; shake
Sick phantoms from a spirit, tuned amiss
　By trouble, and behold his being take
Under the warm world's fresh and fiery kiss
New breath from nature's life and God's creative bliss.

98

"Wouldst thou behold him, bid thy spirit climb
　The clear height specular, whence doubt's deep rift
Doth faint and dwindle, while the full world's chime
　Fuses sad notes unsatisfied, that drift
　Low, ineffectual here! Purge thou and lift
Dim eyes, now disinured, unsensitive
　But to the soul's own twilight, where they sift
O'erfinely inward mood and vision! Give
Thy sense to simple day, look forth and feel and live!

99

"Wouldst thou awake him, learn the purest spell
   Of aspiration! Seem as one akin
To his most perfect dream! and wouldst thou dwell
   Alone in that proud worship, deep within
   The precincts of thy broken nature, twin
To his, with hands by pain and passion skilled,
   And lips so consecrated they should win
His hearing, on love's sacred site rebuild
Thy soul to temple song, and be in him fulfilled!

100

"Howbeit dream not thou shalt repossess
   Lightly or all that vision, human, whole,
Which mirrors, with a larger life express,
   The world's essential image in a soul
   Unsundered. Time's transition now hath stole
Too deep upon thy spirit. Thou must speak
   All its authentic trouble, that control
May ripen inward from the lips that seek
To catch the calm sure utterance of a song antique.

101

"Song is a flower which blossoms on the cleft
  Of some divided life; whose beauty's born,
Or late within a widowed spirit, left
  Alone with memory, dreaming on forlorn
Of the fair past; or from a soul unworn,
Which early, with quick pangs of prophecy,
  Doth tremble onward to a fairer morn,
While want and fulness, fraught with hope and sigh,
Can waken dreams to life sweeter than days which die.

102

"But the rift ever runs and broadens down
  On the perfection of the two lives, wed
By magic of high poesy. His crown
  Of reconcilement withers from the head
Of time. His sweet reprieve doth pass. Unsaid
Is the brief benediction; and dissent,
  Deep, secular, cries on his honour 'dead,'
And doth usurp, upon that fair realm's rent,
The power of song's repose, lord of a world unblent.

103

"And ever must the simple seamless robe
  Rewoven be on later looms; retuned
The lyre to subtler sound; a finer probe,
  More inward, softly laid on nature's wound
  By poet, as by one who hath communed
Deeply with all disease, till he divine
  By wholesome vision, for a soul impugned
In its essential tissue, anodyne,
And large remedial hope.—Look thou and hold it thine!

104

"There with thy spirit, if thou wouldest know
  The hurt and healing of this time's estate,
Watch thou and hearken! If the sound be low
  And inward, there is song articulate;
  There its true heart of action. There high fate
Holds his most secret court and council. There
  Read thou the legend, epic, passionate
Of individual life, reared from despair
Under redemption's law to be fulfilment's heir.

TWO LIVES.

105

" There on the common sea of circumstance
    Let thy sight travel, from the primal stream
Prophetic, over waves of old romance,
    To strange horizons haunted by a gleam
    Of sunny issues infinite! There deem
Amid the relics of a dead world dwell
    Freedom and awe and high effectual dream
To hold thee. There envisage very hell
And heaven, and shape thy sense to feel the spirit's spell.

106

" There shalt thou hear the very pulse of time
    Tremble upon thy being. There behold
The pageantry of all its courses climb
    Across thy vision; catch the echoes rolled
    From its far revolutions, till they mould
Thy motions to their own imperial beat!
    There feel the passion of its purpose fold
    And sway thee, as high powers embattled meet,
To wrestle for thyself, thy freedom or defeat!

107

"There shalt thou touch life's elemental spring;
  Shalt see upon the hidden heart's brief stage
Time's subtle plot, the play of suffering,
  And the sick purpose of a broken age
  Reshapen 'twixt a heavy heritage
And free conception; there proud tragic law
  Hold colloquy with passion; there presage
Luminous of a dawn, whereto we draw,
Purged from ourselves awhile in full prophetic awe.

108

"There in the hollow chamber of the heart,
  Hear the world's spirit breathe, and take the tone
Of thine! Wait thou and listen there apart
  To thy most secret self's confession, grown
  Too full and tremulous to live alone!
Speak as high prophet, on whose tongue no seal
  Is set but reverence! Dare not to disown
Life's infinite commission! Look, reveal
Thy private vision's scope, as one empowered to feel!

109

"There, if thou wouldest fuse in one fair birth
  Loveliness, truth and dream and all desire,
Lend thou thyself, thus strung by time and earth,
  To love, that he may hold thee for his lyre!
  Lend him thy lips, that from the central fire
Of his divinity a flame may fill
  Thy spirit, and his image pass entire,
Essential, where with one creative thrill
He shall sublime thy functions unto his pure will!"

LIFE AND SONG.

METHOUGHT my spirit watched beside sick Time,
   In one brief chamber, where his long-drawn breath,
And heart's faint beating ever seemed to rhyme
   With the slow quiet coming on of death.

And I—so closely was his being blent
   With mine—must helpless wait with him and feel,
While dim shapes in the darkness came and went,
   And spake of life and death and strove to heal.

Grey Science touched and knew that trembling nerve,
   And briefly said, as one that only saw,
" Give thou thyself to nature ! Win and serve
   Her pure force ! Wed thy weakness to her law."

TWO LIVES.

Large Nature softly took him to her breast,
   And placed upon his brow her cooling palm.
She spake, "I bare thee; I will nurse thee; rest;
   Thou shalt outlive me; only learn my calm!"

Young Art bent o'er him with a fresh full kiss,
   That lingered on his lips. A broken gleam,
Or of forgotten or unfashioned bliss,
   Lit his dull vision, while she whispered "Dream!"

Clear Reason pierced with subtle, probing gaze
   Those wandering eyes, and found a pathless soul.
"I will retrace," he said, "thy spirit's ways,
   And show thee where they meet, and life is whole."

Some secret prescience, when their whispering ceased,
   Born of long watching, in my spirit woke;
I flung life's window wide upon the east;
   And sound and vision held me and I spoke—

"I feel the fresh wind teach me his refrain;
   I see the white dawn on my soul ascend;
I hear those voices, beating through my brain,
   Into one song, or mine or morning's, blend."

And then anon there came a matin bell,
  A tone of pure fulfilment, close, more clear—
"Faith is returned to ring for thee night's knell;
  Awake, come forth, oh Time, new life is here!"

And Time arose, and laid his hand in mine;
  And so together from pale dreamful doubt
We passed to worship at the warm world's shrine,
  And found God waiting for us there without.

110

Last winter, moving under mournful pines
  Perpetual, where grey vapours brood and cling,
Sudden, unprisoned from those solemn lines,
  I burst upon the southern world, one thing
  Of sunshine, from the cliffs that shoreward fling
Their crumbled gold, kissed by soft lips of foam,
  Outward and on, till ocean shimmering
Lay crowned with his most pure imperial dome,
And one white headland rose athwart the poet's home.

111

So from the shadow of that dreamy mood
    I passed. I felt a fresh wind rushing purge
My spirit of its stain. Methought I stood
    Full face with man and nature, on the verge
    Of very life. Below a sunlit surge
Seemed to baptize my being. Whole and free,
    I saw the magic isle of song emerge
From loveliness and motion, leaving me
The passion and the peace of God's infinity.

112

I am not mine. No shelter now, nor pause
    Shall hold me from my larger voyage long;
Such visions sway me, such free current draws
    My motions forth. Yet would I make me strong
    One moment by the sight of his clear song,
Which, posted over this low ebbing age,
    Still beacons late and lonely—if among
A new world's waters I might bear presage
Of such another dawn, such hope of harbourage.

113

There lies the sea, whose fulness I would sail.
    Broad-bosomed, solemn, strange, its power has caught
All my heart's craving. Though my song be frail
    For such proud venture, and my soul o'erfraught
    With the deep burden of untravelled thought,
Thus would I seem to beat across the bar
    Of sorrow, straining on with eyes which sought,
Else all unpiloted, to pierce afar
This twilight time, and make one pure perpetual star.

114

I said my spirit darkling and alone
    Seaward was driven by a waft of death;
And after seemed to be more softly blown
    By the calm breeze of love, who followeth
    In his cold wake. But yet should come a breath
Supreme, or be it current, for whose lack
    My purpose were a shoreless thing, beneath
An unsunned heaven, whence I must tremble back
To some forgotten port, or hold a starless track.

115

Scarce were I now content only to sway
  With the last billow on life's face, or drift
Unshapen, dreaming that full flood to-day
  To time's true summit would mechanic lift
  My outlook. But, as one long tossed, would sift
All sound and motion, till my soul divine
  With sure forefeeling, under every shift,
The water's deep set and the wind's design,
For my fulfilment's course—if it were wholly mine.

116

Not wholly mine.—For, ever, as the mist
  Rose from the surface of my soul, I felt
Some subtle influence, mocking analyst,
  Enfold me. Large, effectual it would melt
  Into my purpose. As a power that dwelt
Unlocal, timeless, it could overpeer
  My will's most private motions, and half spelt
Read my whole vision through, and hold it clear,
Till I might dream myself were called to be his seer.

117

Felt I such spirit then, I would invoke
  No lower now; that He, perchance, might use
Me for a voice and mirror, when I woke
  From that high dreaming; that I might not lose
  The authentic power to hold and re-peruse,
And shape His meaning forth in lines unblurred,
  Passionate, palpable; that He might fuse
My whole life's functions to one thing, which heard,
And trembled to His thought, half echo and half word.

118

Oh God—since Thy free spring of growing faith
  So hath unlocked my year from the long east
Of withering doubt—my dim self's sunless wraith—
  If now my nature hath by hope increased
  Unto such fulness, that, although the least
Of consecrated sons of song, I were
  Not all unmeet for this pure temple, priest
Of love and loveliness and truth—oh there
Purge Thou my lips to sing by this imperfect prayer!

119

If there be any isle of loveliness
　Unvisited of man; if any shore
Or haven, looming now with large access
　Mysterious; if far-folded at the core
Of nature new life's promise; if rich lore
Still ripening over time's last human height
　Unharvested; if deep and unwrought ore
Of Thine own revelation—school my sight,
And shape my spirit's course unto Thy Spirit's light.

120

Then were my service high, unsecular;
　Myself were then so wholly wrought and thrilled,
That underneath some unallotted star
　For Thy dear benediction I would build
　This open dome of song. And if I stilled
Briefly the heart of unconsummate time
　With but a dream that it should be fulfilled
By Thy redemption, song itself might rhyme,
A prophecy and part, with Thy full music's chime.

121

Then, in Thy perfect season, were returned
    Song's own fulfilment. Then should leap desire,
Up from life's plenitude, with thoughts which burned
    Clear as white tossing pyramids of fire,
    That from the chestnut's drooping base aspire,
To one pure point. Then I were ripe to sing,
    Musical as this blackbird's liquid lyre,
With the whole world of joy and suffering,
And free the passion taught by my true spirit's spring.

SECOND SPRING.

IF death were not a dateless thing,
    One winter, who would disallow
  All season else and know but "now,"
Since first my sorrow learned to sing,
This should have been a second spring,
    Whose breath is living on my brow.

Since first I looked death in the face,
    Were not his spirit's atmosphere
    So keen, untempered, true and clear,
I might have moved a little space
From his cold presence, by the grace
    And mellow distance of a year.

Oh spring! thou canst not disannul
    My sorrow's cycle. Sudden June
    Why comest thou, thus to commune
With me and April? Wouldst thou dull
The edge of death? Thou art too full;
    We cannot welcome thee so soon.

Yet what if spring might welcome be?
   If daisy low and celandine
   Were come to make my season's sign?
If primrose and anemone
And daffodil were meant for me?
   I hardly dare to hold them mine.

Nay not for me they come, but song,
   Who half mechanic used my brain,
   And measured out this year of pain,
And loitered on my lips, among
The slow months, seeking to prolong
   My sorrow for his own refrain.

I think not song can be a thief,
   To spoil my passion, but true friend,
   Who taketh all I have to lend,
And holdeth all the hope of grief,
For my return to his belief,
   And waiteth at my sorrow's end.

Although I gave but half a soul,
   He sheltered it from sense of time,
   And trained my weakness up to climb
Some height of more serene control,
Whence I should see that life was whole,
   And even learn with death to rhyme.

I lent him, though my heart was loath,
   The savings of my love and hers,
   In faith that, if his hand defers
Fulfilment, I shall garner growth,
And feel that he is blending both
   For some new life, that faintly stirs.

I looked and saw him softly move
   The mask from life, and show beneath
   The purer beauty born of death.
He beckons me to sing and prove
Song is enough to waken love
   In some far May to fuller breath.

Then death were but a dateless thing,
   And love were living on as dear,
   And nature mine, and song more near;
For I have sung and I must sing
As one who sees a second spring,
   And ripens for another year.

CANTO II.

DREAM. DOUBT. NATURE.

TWILIGHT.

I DWELT alone, and loitered ever dreaming,
   Not seeing self, nor knowing things without;
Till life arose and shook my world of seeming,
   And sundered all my being by a doubt.

I looked within, and met, in secret session,
   A spirit disinherited of time;
I saw the fragments of a broken vision;
   I heard the echoes of a vanished chime.

I looked without upon the face of nature,
   And deemed a moment she was more divine;
I found no soul beneath her fairest feature,
   Or only one which seemed to mirror mine.

TWO LIVES.

1

There is a city seated in the eye
   Of my dear recollection. As a dream
It haunts the threshold of my memory,
   Ever a soft and unsubstantial gleam
   Above my spirit's dawn. Far up the stream
Of broadening life it dwells amid the mist;
   There waiting till regret rise and redeem
   Its image from unclearness, lit and kissed
To pure and living truth by love the realist.

2

Love will unmoor for me this wandering boat
   Of fancy, as it tosses late and low,
Set seaward. Love will lightly bid me float
   By his own method back, for all the flow
   Of twenty summers. He will softly blow
Before my senses those grey mysteries
   Of tangled tower and roof, which come and go
   In the fresh magic of that first surmise
Fulfilled with insight born, when feeling faints and dies.

3

I may not linger by the mill, or brood
    Among the meadows, though the pulsing oar
Beats echoing on my heart of solitude;
    I must not loiter aimless on the shore,
    Where the two rivers mingle, where, before
Her pure life melted wholly into mine,
    We spake apart, and listened to the lore
Of undercurrent love; the posted line
Of elms is on me here; beyond my memory's shrine.

4

I move from shadows, as a silent ghost,
    Who cometh, unessential, to enquire
Of his mortality. Old shapes accost
    Half human my full nature's want. Soft fire
    Touches those twisted pillars, and the spire
With the same mellow meaning. Let me roam
    The long street's sunny curve, my dream's desire,
Or haunt the green plot by the one low dome;
Alien, unlocal now; this was thy spirit's home.

5

But still my love, as he that would consort
    With the dear witness of his dead, doth shun
All other vision, but of that cool court,
    Whose shy face cloistered from the common sun,
    And veiled in time's grey texture, softly spun,
Hideth a soul of quietude most pure,
    Unsecular; and, like some sweet pale nun,
Nourishes there, a devotee demure
Of loveliness and dream, calm's perfect temperature.

6

The same brief shadow awes me. The same breath
    Of revelation seems to brood and freight
My vision, as it pauseth there beneath
    Life's inlet through that grey and storied gate,
    Writ over with forgotten hope and fate
Decyphered. There I see dear freedom dwell,
    And softly move to welcome me, or wait
Beyond the enchanted arch, with quiet spell
Weaving her airy tissue to my spirit's cell.

TWO LIVES.

7

I round the sunny turf, a soul alone,
    And mount the dim stair by the silent hall.
Its stillness trembles to the undertone
    Of an unlocal organ's solemn fall
    As ever; and across the panelled wall
Creeps on that mellow and mysterious stain;
    While ghostly now, unindividual,
    Thin voices flit and echo on my brain,
And from the gloom old faces grow and fade again.

8

Again, through some far window subtly hid
    And softly opened by my memory, break
Those early sounds. And sense moves faint amid
    A labyrinth of bells, until they take
    One tone, whereat my whole world leaps awake,
And listens to that tower, which stands apart,
    Like a proud poet, who has felt life shake
    With such tumultuous meaning all his heart,
He must abide alone, built wholly up for art.

9

Again I wander round the garden walk,
    Between the grey wall and the drooping lime;
And dreams live on in fragmentary talk,
    Under the magic of that May's pure prime,
        And light thoughts o'er dim feeling cross and climb,
Where chestnuts hold high tapers shimmering,
    And the beech bronzes; while as chapel chime
Awe briefly lingers, and life seems a thing
Of airy blossoms blown from the soft lips of spring.

10

Oh England, would thy free imperial youth
    Be nurtured for each nobler year, with power
Replenished, purged, this Oxford were in truth
    Pure soil, whereon such life for one fresh hour
        Of unforgotten dawn should dream and flower
For thy ripe fruiting; which at their high source
    Can shape and sweeten, for thy spirit's dower,
New currents, broadening out and down to course
Through thy full beating life, and feed thy nature's force.

11

Here at thy heart of loveliness, a place
    Elect, of high immunity, aloof,
She dwells. And here should souls of thy dear race,
    Unworn, unshapen yet, for thy behoof,
    Holden awhile, beneath some ancient roof,
From sense of all disjointed things, and jar
    Of the loud world, be wrought to time's rich woof
And texture, at his great loom secular,
Which worketh soft and silent under nature's star.

12

Come back! In our full England is no spot,
    Where the benediction of things dear and old
Droppeth so dewy; where grey time doth plot
    And whisper such sweet reason, as, when told,
    With his high schemes incorporate can mould
The wild and mutinous will; where the fresh lore
    And loveliness of nature doth enfold
Young sense so subtly, and through every pore
Of the light spirit creep and nestle at its core.

13

Come back! Oh what if this worn bark of mine,
    O'ertravelled, now a thing at large too long,
Might he reshapen to its dream's design?
    What if this soul itself, remoored among
    Those quiet hills, in the clear depths of song,
Palpable there, more perfect might reread
    Its own reflection, and from nature's tongue
Take up sweet comment on a lonely creed,
Replanted on the past, to ripen from its seed?

14

Come back! For all this longing, I were loath
    To see life post me ever on her brink,
Motionless, musing only on a growth
    Outgrown. For how should I lightly rethink
    Wild thoughts forsworn and sweetened now? Or drink
The dregs of old regret? Or haunt the stair
    Of my ascent? Or even briefly sink
To a forgotten self? who hardly dare
To say if this be dream, redemption or despair.

15

Yet would I once look down, through all the mist
 Of tears and exile, rising thus between
Two lives, oh love, as one who keepeth tryst
 Only with time, upon my city queen,
 Over sweet hawthorn and low Hinksey seen,
From Foxcombe or from Cumnor, where the rim
 Of sense is widened, and the air's soft screen
Breeds such a beauty as doth melt and swim,
While memory tempers truth to dream and vision dim.

RESPICE.

SPIRIT of song,
  Thou pale and formless thing,
Why art thou wandering,
  Thus late and long
Through the wild places of my memory's life,
  Where death is rife?
  Dreamest thou there among
Such seasons thou shalt be fulfilled of strife?
Or shalt ensue the passion of a perfect spring?

For boyhood's simple blossom felt
The world was grey, wherein I dwelt,
A homeless thing, unreconciled.
And youth for joyous June too wild,
Unfolded to a scentless flower,
And stained the face of that free hour.

For wakening thought's first hollow bud
Was troubled by a taint of blood,

TWO LIVES.

And blighted in unfaith's long east;
And love crept on me and increased,
New born of nature's purest breath,
To droop upon the lap of death.

For thou art sprung to meet my mood
Too late, and share my solitude,
Who flowerest from suffering;
My life doth only dream of spring,
And linger down one loveless year;
Oh song, thou canst not shelter here.

    Spirit of life,
  Wander thou with me back
  And clothe me in thy lack;
    Where death is rife,
There can I live and listen there for both,
    Though thou be loath;
  And from far banks of strife
Regather blossoms born for truer growth,
Clasping the skirt of spring, climbing the spirit's track.

For song can keep the primal gleam
Of roses wild, the snowdrop's dream;
And watch the vision of a birth,
When nature, held too near to earth,

Must meet the cloud, and climb and face
New passion's breath, the spirit's space.

And he can bury wild things dead,
And wake the season, where was bred
The hidden germ of free belief;
Can blossom on the lips of grief,
And blend with death, and quickened save
Love's sweetness breathing on the grave.

For song must grow, and he can give
Flowers for regret, and flowering live;
And through the dream that dies behind,
When he hath deeply there divined
Fulfilment's promise, growth's long spring,
Shall reconcile thy lips to sing.

16

Spirits there are so pure, that they embalm
   By their own breath and very effluence
Dead seeming shapes that case them ; whose dear calm
   With consecration's quality doth fence,
   From the common field of circumstantial sense,
A pale perpetual, so sweet it hath
   No flower of wild regret or reticence,
But from encroachment ever holds free path
For life to pasture back on memory's aftermath.

17

Ah me ! And there are souls, which on the face
   Of outward things put off and throughly print
The shadow of themselves. And thus the grace
   Of nature, troubled with a cloudy tint,
   Answers them in her mirror but by hint
And image of infection ; or must bar
   Perfect accèss to high commune, and stint
Her mysteries, pure, free, oracular,
And hold their thought unpurged and heedless feet afar.

18

If such a one there be, as I have dreamt,
    Who treads the hidden ways and underwood
Of my own nature; who hath power to tempt
    My memory back to wander there, and brood
    Below, among the fragments of a mood
Downtrodden; who would climb, as one akin,
    To the true summit of my solitude,
And claim familiar power and place within
Myself, as sad winds sighing from life's origin,

19

Thus would I answer—" Nay, not here, or now
    I know thee, but as him who might have been
Myself. The clouds and sun that overbow
    Low nature's movement, they alone have seen
    Her truth in aspiration's flower. Between
This 'I' and that, fresh seasons came and shook
    My old leaves down to wither there, unclean,
Forgotten round life's root, when I forsook
Thy fellowship for ways, whereon thou shalt not look."

TWO LIVES.

20

"And if I listen, think not thou shalt vaunt
    Thy nakedness; that I would entertain
Confession to but ease thee. Though thou haunt
    The hollow interspaces of a brain,
    Rebuilt for nobler use, with thy refrain
Mechanic; though thou freely canst implead
    My silent past, thou shalt usurp and stain
These lips of song no further than shall breed
Some sense of dead things fallen from a vital seed."

21

"And though within thee, such a soul, unripe,
    Embittered, out of time, misshapen, bare,
Abide, I doubt not, hint and hidden type
    Of the full fruit, whereof I would be heir,
    Which linketh me half-reconciled to share
The memory of thy waste; though mutual
    Henceforth must be our knowledge, yet I were
Loath to behold thee now, or thus recall,
But as a thing outworn, alien, impersonal."

22

So on that spirit still, eyes of reproof
    Peer forth from secret windows in the past,
To hold their visitation. So aloof
    The clear stream of that fresh full world unglassed
    Went gliding by, to find him here at last.
So, as some lonely pine defies the spell
    Of spring, his nature round its growing cast
A darkness and a dream, where it would dwell,
A homeless life with thoughts ripe only to rebel.

23

If there was calm and welcome there, not then
    It took or touched him, dreamful and distraught
Inly with strife. If high upon his ken
    Rose the large world of immemorial thought,
    He was swept fiercely out, a thing unfraught,
From the harbourage of time and hope, to sail
    Long wild ways perilous, a soul who sought,
Under an ancient heaven, grown dim and stale,
A waste sea peopled only by one phantom pale.

24

The breath of strange things, and their graciousness,
   Which brushed his forehead, stayed not to imbue
His being with their magic. No largess
   From life's own liberal hand, no revenue
   Of time enriched him at the first, or drew
His longing forth by high harmonious law.
   No pure fulfilment nurtured him. He grew,
A spirit out of course, as one who saw
Himself athwart the sun, a vision void of awe.

25

Alas! For he had brought a life unclear
   And troubled to the gate of that pure school
Of loveliness. The simple atmosphere
   Of feeling, which should sweep and lightly rule
   The heart of boyhood, seeming but to cool
Its open brow, for him was disendowed
   Of its prime motion. As a sunless pool,
Too often lay his spirit, lonely, proud,
Under the brooding shadow of a formless cloud.

26

For him, unthought, unsevered, with the breath
   Of outward things and nature, there was blent
The whisper of a broken self. Beneath
   The flow of life's free course, some sediment
   Of doubt, some cadence of strange discontent
Fell into sadness. Dull or overstrung
   Grew the fresh nerve of buoyant hours ; forespent
The native pulse of wholesome blood among
Dim footless musings born within a soul too young.

27

So as he wandered down the years of youth
   From the faint hills of childhood, still a mist
Went with him, blurring the bright edge of truth,
   And shape of action. And if warm life kissed
   His soul, yet ever shadows would assist,
To mar the fullness of their meeting. Thence,
   Knowing not self or world, he only wist,
By half-forebodings and a far-off sense
Of things unreconciled, his nature's dissidence.

28

Too young he flowered. And though he moved amid
　His fellows, seeming of them, yet alone,
Ever behind free words and motions hid,
　His spirit dwelt, or wandered homeless, blown
　From the near ways of commune half outgrown,
And from the ken of self, to live with want
　Unshapen, reaping in far fields, unsown,
Vague harvest from his fancy's airy plant,
A countercharm to days, that life would disenchant.

29

Listless he ever paused, upon the brink
　Of two worlds unsubstantial loitering;
Now lost in self, as one who strove to think
　But thought not; now forgetful following
　Life's footsteps, as a half unnoted thing.
But evermore each world would fade and seem
　To leave him briefly touched by vision's wing,
Empty, unrealized beside the stream
Of life—a pathless place for memories of a dream.

30

Not from the laurels of that ancient lore,
    Which lightly crowned his forehead, living shoot
Was grafted on his soul. They hung before
    His eyes, a sapless vision, void of root,
    To wither there or wait his spring. No fruit
Of knowledge nursed his lips to passion. Love,
    Dreamful, unsequelled, dear, irresolute,
Found not a breath to quicken or disprove
The shadowy world wherein he moved or seemed to move.

31

No early bell of reverence rang belief
    On his youth's drowsy ear. No wholesome scope
Of purpose shaped his power forth. No grief
    Shook out his seeming. Never dawn of hope
    Or solemn star of duty rose to cope
A blind will with a law new-born. He trod,
    Unpioneered by prayer, a sunless slope,
The long hours of his twilight period,   [God.
Through time's dim undergrowth, lonely o'erlooked by

32

Only the seasons and their solitude,
    And something of the passion of a place,
And love made local crept upon his mood,
    As kindred of its dream. Ah, they could trace
    Clear record there, and register the face
Of circumstance, the little things of rote,
    Unmemorable, from life's interspace.
And if awhile footless they seemed to float,
Could heal his empty sense with quiet antidote.

33

And still, though unessential, in their track,
    When dreamy fingers from his life's full sheet
Unwrite life's superscription, glimmers back
    Some primal flush of boyhood. Still his feet
    Move through a vision as of something sweet,
Between the ancient arch and village cross,
    And still he wakes and wanders incomplete,
And clasps beneath a dead dream's airy dross
Some residue of golden feeling blent with loss.

DREAM AND DOUBT.

FAR up in the heart of the wild wild moor,
    Where only the earth and the sunshine wist,
Where the free wind whispered his song secure
    To the cloud, as he kept high tryst,
A rivulet rose in a vision pure
    Of purple heather and mist.

Awhile it fretted in wanton foam,
    And its shallows rippled, "Would I were free";
And lightly it longed to broaden and roam
    To the fuller hope of the sea,
As under the vision and ways of home
    Ran the dream of a destiny.

The breath of the wind, from the world's free space,
    With a secret sadness its waters imbued;
The shadow and sun went over its face,
    And mirrored their dream on its mood;
And the dark woods left in its depth a trace
    Of silence and solitude.

TWO LIVES.

Among the meadows, beneath the brink,
   It seemed to murmur, "Would I were still";
It stayed and listened, as though to think,
   By the whirr and the work of the mill;
It heard on its current rise and sink
   The sound of a waking will.

Fresh rivulets ever and falling rain
   Brought motion and life to its being's dearth,
And blent with its ripple a pure refrain
   From the hills and the heaven of its birth;
While deep in its bosom it bore a stain
   From the broken ways of the earth.

The flowers died down on the broadening bank,
   At the touch of the brine and the city's taint;
And nought would blossom but wild growth rank,
   And the wind from the sea was faint;
And the soul of the river was troubled and sank
   In the dregs of a dead restraint.

So the world was dim, and the waters low,
   The deep bed mocking the river's drought;
And the dream of the moor, as a dream long ago,
   Was dying and dying out;
And the sea-dream, born of a ceaseless flow,
   Was lost in the ebb of doubt.

A viewless thing and lonely it dwelt
    With a dead self, shrunken, unpurified;
When its void of bitterness seemed to melt
    In the life of a larger tide,
And it rose to the world's full rim, till it felt
    It was one with a heart more wide.

34

I know not whether such a mood was bred
    Wholly within his nature, lying there
In fallow dream, so waste, untenanted
    Of wholesome thought or motion, it would bear,
    Of its own want and emptiness, rank tare
And wild things misconceived; or whether germ,
    Winged with infection through a fevered air,
From the sick spirit of a time infirm,
Lay brooding deep, to ripen at his season's term.

35

Had her love beckoned to him from the first,
    Had her bright spirit risen, a golden gleam,
On his grey dawn, perchance a nobler thirst
    Had earlier found fulfilment in a stream
    Purer, more calm. His faculty of dream,
Perchance, and will uncentred had been strung
    To the fresh tones of some prophetic theme
Of inspiration opulent; unwrung
His soul by wild regret, his sadness half unsung.

36

But he was set apart, as one recluse,
    Conventual, from the whole world's vision sane,
And the pure breath of love. The very use
    And shaping of an unsubstantial brain
    Seemed but a school predestinate to train
His being for the hour, when the full rite
    Of freedom should baptize him in the pain
And commune of a broken age whose blight
Fell on the hope and passion of its proselyte.

37

For, though a formless mist would ever drape
  His nature, like some wild and lonely heath,
With the twilight of a dreamful mood, and shape
  His spirit to its fancy, deep beneath,
  Brooding, unvital yet, there lay a breath
Of reason, whose keen quality should clear
  The veil from off his brow, leaving a wreath
Of dream to haunt his memory's atmosphere,
And pierce with inward eyes to be his soul's high seer.

38

Wherefore, what time a fair face in the mask
  Of freedom with the mocking eyes of fate,
Blent with his dream and whispered, "Wake and ask!
  I will endow thee with myself; new date
  Thy nature here, and here initiate
Thy feet in my large ways; I will unbar
  For thee illiberal time's last mouldering gate,
And lead thee forth by reason's ample star,
True neophyte of my wide worship secular,"

39

Lightly he heard her welcome, as it broke
    The thread of his dim dreaming, and unwove
Its texture. Then a lawless power arose
    And looked upon her face, and felt the love
    Of her wild beauty clasp his sense, and move
His spirit by its cold fire from the roof
    Of reverence. Then he climbed with her above
A world outworn, downtrodden, and aloof
Sealed his new self and passion in her nature's proof.

40

And there with freedom's phantom for awhile
    He sojourned, seeming to her soul akin.
But she, lest the full world should reconcile
    His lonely nature, and a new love win
    His vision back from her, a pale thing, thin,
Impalpable, wrought, with a subtle spell,
    Such madness of denial deep within
His will, she deemed that he must ever dwell
Wholly in her wild love, and be life's infidel.

41

For the dear growth and use of sheltering time,
    Which, in the fresh hour of the spirit's spring,
From the soft soil of life should sunward climb
    And clothe its bareness, was for him a thing
    Extrinsic. He had felt no fibres cling
To his true sense, or clamber to his heart,
    That sweet thoughts might have nestled there to sing,
Nor flower of aspiration rise to thwart
The passion of a soul, which strove to be apart.

42

Though it was spring, the dead and hollow rind
    Of faith and reverence, as the full sap grew
With lawless feeling, and a barren wind
    From the empty east of reason rose and blew
    About his being, fell, a withered strew
Before a naked soul. And he could face
    A bleak world lightly thus, and wander through
The leafless autumn ways of liberal space,
Haunted with broken gleams of unregarded grace.

43

So by that wild wind, risen from a rift
  Now deepening down upon a self unknown,
And rhyming with its solitary drift
  To a void dreaming, he was fiercely blown.
  He wandered forth, until he stood alone
On waste heights, which he deemed the very verge
  Of the wide future, whence the voice and tone
Of time's unshapen music should emerge,
And he should see the vision of full freedom's surge.

44

And there he felt his spirit's motions form,
  And blend with waves of the long after-roll,
Unspent, which followed from that southern storm
  Of liberty, that shook time's strong control
  From the light helm of France, but on the mole
Of our too solid England evermore
  Broke foaming. Yet around each restless soul,
Unlulled it beateth inly, till the lore
Of revolution echoes on its silent shore.

45

There was a poet then, the very breath
   Of pure rebellion, whose keen nature kissed
By the fiery sun of freedom, like a wreath
   Of purple cloud, or unessential mist
   Haunted life's peaks ; a soul idealist,
So elemental, light, timeless and rare,
   He seemed a thing disbodied, to resist
Earth's pressure, and to soar and linger there,
Breathing aloof the vision of his private air.

46

And if our low sense lost his viewless flight,
   And deemed his sweet note something overshrill,
Heard through the ether of unlocal height,
   Where wild lips waited not for time to fill
   The measure of their music, it could thrill
And pierce life's purest fibre, such a string,
   Strained to the tension of a tameless will,
Lay quick within his spirit, quivering
To nature's finest breath, and bade her secret sing.

TWO LIVES.

47

And though anon his vision floated thin
　As dreamful cloud across the breathless blue,
A pale soul, half monastic, half akin
　To earth, his passion, as it melted, drew
　The veil from off a far and sunny view
Of a beauty and a brotherhood more free,
　And from a dawning, dyed to the full hue
Of his own faith and golden phantasy,
Sank in the purple bosom of a southern sea.

48

Shelley, for such as thou there is no birth,
　Nor death. No petty months or years compute
The measure of thy young and living worth.
　They cannot touch the undated attribute
　Of thy free dreamful music, or transmute
Its fashion. Would that now thy spirit's power,
　Grafted anew on quick time's growing root,
From this ripe century fulfilled might flower,
And mellow in life's sun to song's most perfect hour.

49

Though on the lap of Rome thy lonely dust
  Be hidden, and thy frame, which felt the fire
And elemental surge, be held in trust
  By time's most central earth; though now, entire
  By death and God's purgation, doth aspire
Thy soul to breathe his ether's height, and draw
  Fulfilment's music from thy broken lyre,
Restrung to tones of love's essential law,
And bend for the last wreath of consecrating awe,

50

Yet here in this fair Oxford late shall burn
  A breath of thy clear spirit, to illume
Grey wall and grassy plot for thy return;
  Yet calm's art's carven grief shall disentomb
  Some shape of thy free presence; shall consume
On its pale marble pyre all memories wild
  With God's own pity; yet shall live perfume
Of youth, which here had blossomed, unexiled,
More sweet, of passion dead, of sad things reconciled.

SONG AND LIFE.

LIFE, half awakened from a dream,
　　Arose and wandered out among
The shadows of the things that seem,
　　And stood before the house of song.

He cried, "Oh bid me now behold
　　The beauty I can half divine!
Show me thyself, that I may fold
　　Thy nature's fullness into mine!"

Lightly his spirit passed within;
　　He only felt his vision kissed
By cold lips unto dream akin;
　　His longing met a thing of mist.

And thin and far there seemed to float,
　　In formless waves, her tone's refrain;
"Thou canst not catch my nature's note
　　Till passion be attuned to pain."

"Thou shalt not see my love's true face,
　Till sight be purged for prophecy;
Nor meet my being's full embrace,
　Till sense and self broaden and die."

"No hand can touch my heart's high key,
　But love first tremble down the nerve;
Or my pure pulse of mystery,
　Till it be strung to death's reserve."

"First love—I would not half reveal
　Myself to such a callow thing;
Last love—when thou art fledged to feel—
　Shall in long seasons learn to sing."

"Go forth from me! Until thou climb
　My spirit's height, my lips defer
Song's consummation. Live with time!
　Wouldst thou be my true worshipper."

"Go forth! I know thee not. Know thou
　Thyself and nature! Feel, forget!
My kiss shall be upon thy brow,
　When hope hath ripened from regret."

"Grow thou for me, till life be twain,
 By sin, unfaith, reflection, law!
Grow thou to me, till love regain
 New shapes of vision void of flaw!"

"If thou wouldst see in song no wraith,
 Awake and clamber to the noon
Of knowledge! Wing thy feet with faith!
 And clothe thee for my far commune!"

"If thou wouldst win my perfect soul,
 Through day and night's full period
Sweep to the star, that maketh whole,
 And burneth on the breast of God!"

"Come back! For thee, unwooed awhile,
 Holding the deeper dream of eve,
I wait to crown and reconcile;
 Come back! I wait. Oh love, believe!"

"Come back! Behold and clasp my life,
 Myself, to make thee calm and strong!
At eve fulfilment flowers from strife,
 And blends thy being into song."

51

So he against a misconceivèd wraith
  Of most majestic time, that he might pledge
His spirit to the power of that fierce faith
  Of nothingness, turned the untempered edge
  Of his unproven thought. No awe might hedge
With its mute sanction the high-templed past,
  Or the pure infinite from sacrilege
Of wild lips and rude reason, as he cast
Their fragments at his feet, a blind iconoclast.

52

But though his homeless spirit sojourned long
  Beside the empty desecrated shrine
Of a worship, where he sheltered not, no song
  Built him new fabric for his soul's design;
  No free faith in a joyous youth divine
Of things and years regenerate rose to cope
  The void he wrought around him; the red wine
Of freedom flushed not to its vision's scope
The cold thoughts of a heart, uncoursed by power of hope.

53

Not love, whose sovereign function doth enlarge
  To its own nature's breadth and plenitude
The private spirit, and with fullness charge
  Its empty frame of want, might yet intrude
  On his soul's waste and solitary mood.
No voice of dear devotion's reverence
  Stirred him. No breath of fellowship imbued
His being with the world's fine effluence,
Or blent with outward things a wild sequestered sense.

54

Unrapt he moved and dreamful, as he felt
  Proud purpose ripen on him to refuse
Life's full endowment; and familiar dwelt
  With solitude, as one who might not lose
  The shadow of his soul. He seemed to muse
In commune with a presence, formless, faint,
  Whose image he must daily reperuse,
Till the red hour of shame should rise and paint
His twilight unto truth, and slowly thus acquaint

55

His spirit with its need, what time, the night
    Of fancy fading, he should coldly trace,
In the long grey dawn of disillusion's light,
    The blank and passionless penury of space,
    Hearing the sad winds through the ruined place
Of a nature, broken, disinherited,
    Sweep sighing evermore, and see full face
A self so bare, its vision should have bred
Some high conception's seed, some dream of hope not dead.

56

Only to nature would his longing turn,
    And wander through her ways. For her largess,
Kinder than any wage that he might earn
    By his sad service, would fulfil and bless
    Briefly his soul. There could he half confess
For her sweet absolution all his gloom,
    Half hear the secret of his emptiness
In her pure silence, blent with such perfume
As love's dear presence breathes within a darkened room.

57

But though she soothed him, she might hardly heal
　His sickness, until pain's pure truth should wake
His apathy to day and power to feel,
　And probe its hollow want; till life should shake
　His being free, and love's own season break
The waste fields of his dreamful impotence
　With fruitful passion; till regret should make
A deep home in his nature's dissidence,
And sweet thoughts sow anew the wildness of his sense.

58

And thus he wandered on, as one who dreamt,
　Among the dead leaves of life's underwood,
A thing half lost in sunless self-contempt,
　Passionless and unreal. Then he stood
　At the broken ways of that deep solitude;
And lingering aimless there, he caught between
　The shadows falling from a bitter mood,
And a self hidden by a misty screen,
The glow of passion's quest for some far height half seen.

59

And thus there rose upon his lonely thirst
    The fresh strong love of fair philosophy,
And swayed him. Not as nature subtly nursed
    His mood to her calm tones and melody,
    But with the troubled music of the sea
She drew his blind steps to the world's high brink,
    And showed him all the hope of vision, free
To clear life's furthest rim; and bade him drink
Of her wide wisdom's draught, and in her fullness sink.

60

But winds, that spake not half her spirit forth,
    Filled the light want of an unladen soul,
And swept it wildly out to reason's north,
    Mocking belief in full life's rounded whole
    With the shoreless vision of some hidden pole
Of merest nothingness, whose one cold star
    Trode down the last light of time's long control,
And held him with clear passion ocular,
And fashioned to its scope his broadening course afar.

61

From the low dream, where half his nature dwelt
  Amid the mists, that seemed to line and wreathe
The valley of his viewless life, he felt
  His longing drawn. He saw free hands unsheathe
  Keen faculties he knew not. He could breathe
Fresh upland scenes, and clamber to an air,
  Whence he beheld far down dim fancies seethe
Formless, and widely clasped, although it were
Only an outward shape, whose thought he might not share.

62

For how should freedom's aweless passion fledge
  A reason callow yet for the full flight
And native pitch of its pure privilege?
  How, if it were but nature's proselyte,
  Ordain it to true function? How should sight,
Unsunned by time or love's tuition, soar
  Prophetic to the world's imperial height?
Or pierce, by faith unwhetted, to the core
And common heart of things, and hold life's perfect lore?

63

It was a soulless and unreverend truth,
　To whose grey temple he would coldly turn
A novice and unconsecrated youth.
　It was her outer court, where he could learn
　Her tongue and ritual only; not discern
Through hard forms of mechanic vision, freed
　From sense, that fiery spirit, which must burn
All functions in one ministry to feed
Her full pure worship's hearth, her high prophetic creed.

64

Such power was hers, as, working there aloof
　Upon the dim forge of a dreamy brain,
Shaped forth a reason, impotent at proof
　Of passion, and untempered to the strain
　Of life. Therewith she strove to arm and train
To her keen nature's use and lead him out
　By empty ways, that on the full world's plain
His spirit renegade might rise and flout
The blank and pallid banners of embattled doubt.

65

So, when his nature should have seen new birth,
  Unfaith, false high priest of a soulless age,
Breathed on him and baptized him unto earth,
  And disendowed him of all heritage
  Of hope. Dead hands of reason came to cage
The unshapen spirit in the barren womb
  Of nothingness. His dreamful spring's presage
Was warped by winds untimely, and the bloom,
That might have been, was wasted in a grey world's gloom.

66

For first love drew him wholly to that school,
  Whose hollow frame of liberty doth mould
Thought's young life and light motions to a rule
  Mechanic; whose half lore can briefly hold
  The allegiance of a nature unenrolled
By love or time's prevention; which doth pare
  To penury of sense the spirit's gold,
Mocking its passion with a promise bare,
And feed full longing's growth with dead fruits of despair.

67

And reason, which had learnt not yet to probe
  The leanness of a faculty, unripe,
Empty, unnurtured, plucked time's woven robe
    From the warm world, and stripped it to the type
    Of his own bareness; and would blindly wipe
The deep-lined purpose of a soul akin
    Out from life's forehead, while the poor shrill pipe
Of doubt and disillusion's music thin
Piercing awoke his dream to their sad discipline.

68

Thus was he sworn to rebel thoughts, which rose
    From that void longing. Through the inmost gate
Of life they broke imperious, to depose
    The high proud spirit from its royal state
    And motion large. Thus passion leagued with fate
Crept on its pale of power in the guise
    Of freedom. Thus it sank, a delegate
Of their blind plotting; and its prophecies
Put on their hollow voice, the vision of their eyes.

69

Alone he stood before the dull dawn. Lost
    In vision grey, went out one lingering gleam
Of awe. God was an unauthentic ghost
    Of twilight knowledge now; and self did seem
    A false shape, misbegotten in a dream
Of dim sense, blurring by its very breath
    The windows of wide truth; till as a stream
Wandering by cold December ways beneath
A leafless world, be mirrored nought but nature's death.

70

So scant a worship lured him to the porch
    Of high reflection. Such dank winds of doubt
Blew shivering round his soul's half-kindled torch,
    Which flung deep shadows on the life without.
    Such passion of denial, more devout,
More meagre, straiter than the very mind   [drought
    Which mastered him, and mocked his dream-world's
With the mirage of reason, strove to bind
Its veil across his brow and visions undivined.

71

Such hard pale rays of reason, seen betwixt
    Dream's twilight and the rise of love's red star,
Filling the void of revelation, fixed
    His eyes, enfranchised from all vision far
    Of things sublime. Such awe discipular
Led him to that keen spirit passionless,
    Who was the cold saint of his calendar,
And fired his fiercer worship to confess
Unfaith's whole iron form and creed of emptiness.

72

That was a spirit loftier and more broad
    Than his lean nurture—Mill. His motions left
By man's more liberal method the low road
    He paved through nature's plain; and spreading cleft
    The cell of system. Subtler than the weft
Of reason, life's large human residue
    Worked on his vision, till, by noble theft
Of thought unearned, engrafted, he outgrew
Himself for God's late hope and high fulfilment's view.

GROWTH.

OH far and low
    In the moor's brown fold,
Where the wind doth know
    And the sun behold,
A lonely gentian sprang and grew,
And blossomed in autumn long ago,
To be one perfect bell of pure deep-throated blue.

Oh bare and free,
    As the waste bleak moor,
Would the large world be
    In a vision poor,
As a shy flower dwelt with its dream alone,
And grew as a thing that should only see,
And life was void and viewless, and the mist was blown.

Oh deep and near,
    Through fibre and vein,

Till it seemed to hear,
  There rose a refrain
Low down from the heart and the lap of the earth,
  That clasped its memory's root unclear,
And drew its nature back to blend with ways of birth.

Oh wide and full,
  On the lips of the wind,
In passion and lull,
  From life's large mind,
The breath of the world would whisper there,
  And nature's severance half annul,
And fill a lonely sense with secrets life must share.

Oh high and true,
  The face of the sun
Looked down and through,
  And the world was one;
And its life was lifted to breathe the whole,
  And blent with the heaven's perfect blue;
And love and song came by and planted it in their soul.

73

From the dim places, where alone he dreamt,
  That phantom of false reason drew his soul
Apart. He felt its subtle power tempt
  With promise of one world's imperial whole,
  And of self seated in proud truth's control,
His solitary thought; while keen more clear,
  Through that cold commune, to time's very goal
His vision seemed to reach—such atmosphere
Revealed life's barren range to sense its only seer.

74

For him that phantom wore two faces—One,
  The brow of liberty, and fruitful eye,
Broadening that knowledge, as a perfect sun,
  Might meet and seal its vision's prophecy;
  One with lean lips ascetic would belie
Its own fulfilment, as a thing that knows
  No touch of liberal truth's large charity,
And pressed penurious hands, thus to foreclose
Hope, that by life's whole method to completion grows.

75

It spake to him as with two voices—" School
    The outlook of thy spirit vagabond,
And trammel up its issues to the rule
    Of my cold abstinence. And if beyond
    The low horizon of my love, unconned
And shoreless oceans haunt thee, thou shalt drown
    Their sighing music, when at my free wand
Thou hearest time's high palace ruin down,
And from its sound and silence win new wisdom's crown."

76

But though it wakened from their lonely trance
    Those brooding eyes, it might not wholly sate
Or tame by such spare reason's sustenance
    Their speculative vision new, or bate
    Their edge of longing with blank walls of fate.
Still want unshapen sojourned on to breed
    A far-off passion for a future mate
More human. On his waste yet fell a seed,
Blown out by nature's breath, to ripen for her creed.

77

So was he driven to the wilderness,
 The spirit's desert of denial, strown
With dead thoughts. There transition's troubled stress
 Passed on him, as he dwelt and strave alone.
 For God was not, and man a thing misgrown,
Unkindred. There he nursed an empty mood
 Mid fragments of a fallow life, self-sown
With wild regrets unjoyous, seeking food
Only on nature's breast and heart of solitude.

78

Oh nature knoweth revelations twain,
 Shown to man's spirit, shapen on its mould.
For loveliness is seated suzerain
 On her broad bosom, where her heart doth hold
 Such prophecy of love, as shall unfold
Full comfort and free vision's hope. But law
 Dwelleth below her vesture, seeming cold,
 And looketh forth, as who would half withdraw,
Half clasp the veil that lieth on the face of awe.

79

But on his wayward spirit dawned apart,
    Diverse, her visions twain, unreconciled
By God's large method yet. That—to his heart
    Had lightly stolen with transition mild,
    Sheltered him from himself; had wept and smiled
With his own shadowy mood, a minister
    Breathing about his sense things sweet and wild,
Whose far fruition she would half defer,
Till his full soul were ripe to turn interpreter.

80

More sudden this—between the dreamy bud
    Of love's long brooding commune, and the flower
Of insight proven, ere life's wholesome blood   [power
    Had coursed his waking brain—with cold light's
    Flashed through the inlet of an empty hour,
And showed his thought an image of false fruit,
    The lean reflection of a spirit, sour,
Unshapen, as her primal attribute,
Slurring her season's growth, and deep diviner root.

81

From the fair presence, which familiar dwelt
    Beside him, blent with dreamful memories,
And pregnant with the hope of lore unfelt,
    His passion held aloof impatient eyes.
He waited not on her low prophecies
    Of that ripe hour, wherein he should return
    For the fulfilment of a love more wise
Than wisdom loveless, and at last discern
Her beauty wake to thought, and into worship burn.

82

And so was nature grown God's substitute,
    For him a thing unspiritual, whose face,
Swept by a wind of death, seemed to transmute
    Life's full suggestion and free soul of grace,
    And human kinship, bred of sweet embrace,
To one mere shape of power. And she that stilled
    And fired his sense with beauty, and to space
Touched his light spirit, held him cabined, chilled,
In law's thin icy grasp, passionless, unfulfilled.

83

For as he doubted, fallen from the faith,
  The large hope and high service catholic
Of whole consummate reason, a cold wraith
  Of the full life of science rose to trick
  The empty passion of time's heretic.
Her free and hollow front of seeming drew
  His spirit, homeless, unallotted, sick
Of twilight shadows, to her retinue,
And showed her worship's home, and nature's vision new.

84

All sense he stood. Before her proselyte,
  Pointing his reverence unto nature's east
Of orbing knowledge, clear upon the site
  Of ruined reason and of faith deceased,
  Rose her proud temple's dome. And time her priest,
Self-consecrate, on life's high pedestal
  Seemed to unveil truth's image, slowly pieced
And carven from earth's quarried heart, and call
New worlds to kneel beneath her shrine material.

85

That marble shape, with soulless eyes of death,
  Unmystic, took his reason recreant.
And, under such chill benediction's breath,
  Old chimes of worship faded, as her chant
  Rolled inward with a burden jubilant—
"Now is God fallen, fallen! Come, return
  To earth! To me her chief hierophant
Hearken! On her low altar only burn!
The vision of thyself in service there discern!"

86

Then was he nature's—not as those that feel
  The passion of her presence, simply blent
With dear allegiance, work and calmly seal
  Their consecration; such as dwell content
  Wholly to walk her ways, and listen bent
Over her breath, till love unfold in lore,
  And grow within them to ripe argument
Organic; such as live and brood and pore,
Till her own face interpret all her being's core—

87

But so put forth a fierce impatient hand
  To pluck from off her forehead high result,
Untimely, sudden, that the mystic band
  Of awe, wherewith full human love adult
  Girdles her revelation's living cult,
Fell loosened for his sense; and dreamed that there
  Should knowledge dwell familiar, and exult
Thus to behold, in very vision bare,
False truth of naked nature through life's fuller wear.

88

Whether some elemental touch of earth,
  Recurrent, trembled through his blood, and won
Upon the human pulse; or very dearth
  Over the void of fancy subtly spun
  Some wild dim formless longing to be one
With outward things; or passion would peruse
  Nature's new world romantic, so to shun
Too real self, and by her charm to lose
The phantom of a past, wherewith he might not fuse;

89

Or whether, chief, the broken restless nerve
    Of a sick spirit, which in part foresaw
The pain of waking loom afar, would swerve
    And start from the sharp healing of its flaw
    By shame resurgent; but would turn and draw,
Still dreaming, absolution's anodyne
    From unreproachful lips of soulless law,
I say not—only came no dawn divine
To that lean nature's life, which would with his entwine.

90

How else should the free spirit, human, whole,
    Consent to wander back on nature's waste?
How, treading down the hope of its high goal,
    Till vision's faculty be half effaced,
    Averse, can haunt its upward stream, retraced
To the wild blank barren issue, whence it rose?
    And stand a surface thing, shallow, abased,
As who would linger there, and there foreclose
All dream of deepening quest, which to God's ocean grows?

91

How else behold fate's finger only carve
  The soul's full image after nature's frame
Unvital, fleshless? How decline and starve
  The spirit of its sustenance, and maim
    Its motions free? How else should life disclaim
True birth, deeming itself a thing misbred
  By aspiration? How put off high aim
Prophetic? How, self-disinherited,
Reclothe an inward want in dream of worlds long dead?

92

How bear to be an atom-waif of time,
  Tossed out upon the foam of shoreless chance,
Mocked with a sky, whose void its motions climb
  In vain? To see the twilight of its trance
    Break in a shadowy self, that circumstance
Usurpeth for his mirror? To be lift
  On dream's free topmost wave of far advance,
Only to feel below life's backward drift,
Only divine the vision of its own deep rift?

TWO LIVES.

93

Ay—to such issue was his spirit wrought;
   Whose barren soil, unstirred by higher need,
Untilled of time; whose solitary thought
   And wild sense mated to an empty creed,
   Unfertile, the rich promise of that seed,
Dropped on quick waiting life, as pollen's gold,
   By him, whose patient vision seemed to breed
With ripe creative magic, and to mould
New life in nature's lap, new flowers that yet unfold.

94

Darwin—There grew a large and simple life,
   A spirit touched to nobler strains and use,
Than was begotten ever in the strife
   Of blind worlds. There a loyal soul, recluse,
   So listened to full nature's heart profuse,
Her silence took his voice; her soul, unloath,
   As to pure priest's true question, learned to loose
The veil from off the secret of her growth,
And sight's long service blent to tongue prophetic both.

95

Broad-browed, benignant—then on thee the calm
    Of nature fell, and now death's attribute
Of consecration. But must life embalm,
    Deep in this century of thine, the root
    And freshness of thy power. Though time transmute
And choose, the mellow methods of his law,
    Rounding and ripening for fulfilment's fruit,
Linked unto thee, as one elect, shall draw
Through thee to springs diviner than thy spirit saw.

96

But he, whose nature yet was poor, unripe
    For late fulfilment's hour, nor caught the clue
Of aspiration's spring, flung out the type
    Of his own want upon the full world's view.
    And there he dreamed his vision should ensue,
Far off, life's limit in some soulless germ;
    Nor yet foresaw the free ways which outgrew
Growth unprophetic, flowering to affirm
Spirit and self thereafter in true season's term.

97

For, ever backward, by the shadows cast
　From a broken self's reflection, out of rhyme
With life, some formless passion of the past,
　Some longing void for elemental prime,
　Like phantoms, lured him down the steps of time,
To watch its travail, till all sense of birth
　Died in the long transition, whence would climb,
From secular gestation of the earth,
Wind and illusion's shape, to clothe the spirit's dearth.

98

And there, as one half willing to be lost,
　He was content to roam beneath the roof
Of opening ages. There forgot the ghost
　Of self in some far dream of proud disproof.
　And there, though life's large spirit stood aloof,
Strove to behold her barren frame conceive
　All growth, that, through time's vesture and the woof
Of the rich world, wild sense might wholly cleave
To such bare truth, whose tissue law's dead fingers weave.

99

Wherefore was life a shoreless thing, between
    Two worlds of mist, whose grey and spectral gloom
Would ever hang one cold and widening screen
    Across the spirit's quest; and power a doom,
    At whose dim fiat law should half illume
Death's way for shadowy souls, that upward strive;
    And growth a curse misgotten of the womb
Of nothing, whose deep oppositions rive,
And lure time's own elect to clamber and survive.

100

Wherefore was nature set, one soulless norm,
    Whereto his world was straitened; who could fuse
Lightly life's full rich metal in her form
    Mechanic, with wild reason's heat; and lose
    True growth's high law, watching her motions choose,
Which chose not nor were shapen of presage,
    From lavish chance, seeds she would blindly use,
Sown on the mystic lap of heritage,
Till time's mere method seemed to take the spirit's stage.

101

Yet was his being led beyond the marge
   Of private vision. Yet he heard within
The beat and motion of a life more large
   Rise echoing on his nature, as akin
   Recurrent through the blood. Yet seemed to win
Space and one path, to turn and reascend
   Late from the ways of growth and origin,
And there, regathering time's true blossoms, blend
With whole fulfilment's view, and face the spirit's end.

102

Three lords in nature rule—art, science, song—
   Shaping her service to their passion's food;
Three lovers, unto whom she doth belong,
   As one that seeketh only to be wooed;
   Three ministers which wait upon her mood;
Three priests that bless her elemental ore
   To purest use; three spirits that do brood
Over her silence, till her secret's core
Rise to prophetic lips and perfect vision's lore.

103

Three such he knew, or felt their primal breath
    Of inspiration move upon his face
And nature's, with a power which passed beneath
    Slowly to love. Thereof one would enlace
    His motions with her law and wide embrace;
One, with rich vision warm, and softly paint
    Across a grey life's free and shadowy space
    Loveliness; one would answer and acquaint
His mood with hers, and briefly heal division's taint.

104

For he would bathe in streams of fairest art,
    Which image nature, lonely sense, and view
Self in his mirror, whose proud soul apart,
    Wholly express in form, to nature grew
    In stolen converse, till it sunlike drew,
Through his fine vision's free prophetic mist,
    Her beauty forth, more fused, more subtly true,
    Reshapen, mellowed, wider than she wist,—
Turner—by love's long use her ripe impressionist.

CUI BONO.

A WILD rose over the the rivulet bent,
   The wind was a whisper and half a sigh,
And the hum of the bee with its life was blent,
   And the cloud went shadowless by,
   Heigho! And the sun was high.

And the rose, as a thing in a formless dream,
   The shape of her vision and self would trace;
And fairer more faint in the tremulous stream
   She met with her mirrored grace,
   Heigho! and the sun's full face.

She hearkened awhile as a soul alone,
   But she only heard in the hum of the bee,
"Thy life in the lap of the earth was grown
   Thy beauty was made for me."
   Heigho! And the sun could see.

And her life was sad, and the soft lips curled,
   And the grey cloud grew, till her heart would close,
But the song of the wind went over the world,
   And bore the breath of the rose;
   Heigho! And the sun he knows.

105

Lonely he stood, as one who would escape
   Himself and life's clear mirror. Now in dream
His spirit moved aloof, and sought to drape
   Sadness in airy sense, or brooding seem
   To lose all things authentic in the gleam
Of fancy. Now he woke and wandered out
   And bathed a troubled self in nature's stream
Of loveliness. And now in nature's drought
Haunted the hollow waste and empty ways of doubt.

106

And there with wild and shapeless things he dwelt,
  The free and mystic wind, brown moor and wold,
Cloud and grey sea, whose fellowship would melt
  Into his mood, and soothe and softly fold
  His longing. Or, as striving to withhold
A shy unshapen spirit, which would face
  Such dreamful emptiness, from the true mould
Of time, by barren reason wrought a space,
Where he might be apart, a silent, soulless place.

107

And yet anon his being seemed restrung
  To life's true tension. He would catch and blend
With the air of common things; or lightly flung
  His passion on the full world's arms; would lend
  Himself to wave and river; buoyant bend
To the oar's pulsing motion and refrain
  His open youth; or, half fulfilled in friend,
Sweep the new surface of a trackless brain,
Breathing new nature's breath, and sweet life's vision sane.

108

But evermore the stream of outward sense
　　Was shot and ruffled by the wind of thought.
Ever emotion, touched with transience,
　　Was broken, blurred, as, floating thus unfraught,
　　Helmless through shadowy woods, his hearing caught
Some undercurrent tone, that ever sighed
　　Nearer; the whisper of a life which sought
To wear upon his nature and divide
His spirit for itself, and deepen to its tide.

109

And evermore a passion analyst
　　Drew him to wander in the ways unclear,
Where life is haunted by the spirit's mist,
　　As deeming in that twilight atmosphere
　　Reason unreverent should be the seer
Of time's true vision, or as one akin
　　In mood.　Then, unprophetic, saw appear,
As rose two pure stars, love and law, within,
Flung on a riven soul the shadowed form of sin.

110

And thus song found his season; not to nerve
  Or ripen then. But with the light impress
Of spring, it planted there some pure reserve
  Amid wild paths, that love might seek accèss
  Later; there heard his silence half confess
The secret of his dreamful mood; and strawed
  Softly before the feet of bitterness
Young buds of nature, till the name of " Maud "
Sank on a lonely sense, half sweetened and half awed.

111

And though far other love should subtly probe
  With shame and aspiration's power the hurt
Hid in his nature; other thought unrobe
  The bareness of his soul, and with the skirt
  Of time's true raiment cover and convert
Its empty passion; other life recharge
  His life unladen, till the free world, girt
At last with God's horizon, should enlarge
A vision more divine to deep fulfilment's marge;

112

The light wind of that song, which purely shook
    And freshened his sad season at the first,
Is wafted back, and round some sheltered nook
    Of ripened fancy, by its sweetness nursed,
    Wanders familiar, as a thing rehearsed
To love's dear habit. Still its echoes call
    Through far faint chambers to a soul immersed
In its own vision, rhythmic, musical,
And footless haunt his mood, and softly beat and fall.

113

Oh now more softly, seeing that dull death
    Hath frozen up song's summer current, whence
Such sweet waves wandered, pulsing with the breath
    Of love and nature's west, through audience
    Of our free world, waking its fuller sense;
Seeing that his chill weight hath power to numb
    Wholly the heart of music, and condense
The spirit's supple air, till no sounds come,
And sorrow heareth not, and the lips of life are dumb.

114

Oh grey October dawn, thou comest back,
  With autumn's pause, that cold room and the rote
Of common things recurrent, of whose track
  All sense were faded, but for death's deep note
  Then graven. Yet, methinks, I hear him quote
One question from the lips of waiting dread,
  Touching that life, until one answer smote
The silence, and the chestnut witherèd,
And the thin aspen's leaves listened and whispered "Dead."

115

For, even as I spake of nature's speech,
  Hearing two voices, seeing visions twain
Of law and loveliness, and watched them reach
  Apart, and with spring passion purge or stain
  An unripened spirit's free and formless brain,
He, at whose song I felt her sweet sap stir,
  Now rising to my season's own refrain,
Who to my wild sense was interpreter,
Passed, and I knew him blent with silence and with her.

116

Blent—living, dead—his spirit still shall fuse
    Her revelation's fullness, now more dear.
For this fair England's face shall never lose
    Fresh beauty, painted by his vision clear,
    Who gazed through human art's true atmosphere,
Till to his pure constraint, as love would brood
    Prophetic, she uncovered for her seer
Bosom and silent soul and mystic mood,
With his fine passion's breath and subtle form imbued.

117

And I, what time the slow hours watched the ebb
    Of his broad life, was wandering, as before,
By this brown channel, woven in the web
    Of his melodious magic evermore;
    Where, fringed with glamour from that purple shore
Of legend, sea and Severn, to and fro,
    Beating and blending with his sorrow's lore,
Part the faint fields of passion long ago,
And bathe my love's fresh summers in their fall and flow.

118

Oh love ! Along those shores, that autumn dusk,
   While at thy children's feet the dreamy foam
Rose lapping, outward, down, from Wye to Usk,
   By the haven of his memory and each holm,
   Our quiet stream, the Quantock where we clomb,
To the free breath and utmost blue of Morte
   Ran clear my longing's current, which must roam
Ever to love's last issue, and consort
With soulless things awhile, and wait my passion's port.

119

Come back ! Fulfilment's touch with one red flush
   Of sunset shamed brown waters, and there fell
On woodland head and harbour autumn's hush,
   Cool mist and calm. Beneath that ripe hour's spell,
   From brimming bar and westering sail's farewell,
Home by the quarried cliff and haunting moan
   Of sliding ships we followed that soft swell,
Whereon by God's breath he was seaward blown,
For me dead love rose flooding into song, alone.

120

They told me song was dying, dead; such song
    As hears the authentic heart of growing time,
And all its passion's music beat among
    The secret places of his power, then climb,
    With the true pulse of its essential prime,
And flush his faculties, and wake his word
    On lips of love creative, whose full chime,
Echoing back and blending with life's chord,
So maketh free and whole—the breath of beauty's lord.

121

And ever was their muttered half lament
    Lost in his music, whose high laurelled brow
Rose, as some island peak, sole, eminent,
    With immemorial ease doth overbow
    The level ways of petty life. But now,
Rhyming with their presage, the mist of death
    Of his large custom's awe would disendow
Our sense, and on that forehead set his wreath,
Purer than any song we whisper here beneath.

TWO LIVES.

122

Dead! Since the courier lightning, who doth serve
    The public scope of grief, with that first spark
Flashed round the fibres of the world's quick nerve,
    And made a space and silence in the dark,
    Loosening elemental tears, whose mark
Shall burn upon time's brain one deepening date,
    Must we, who saw so large a soul embark
Calmly on his last voyage, haunt the gate,
And range the house of song, sorrowful, desolate.

123

The black sail dwindles down the year. Unbuoyed
    By vision, dumb and listless on the verge
We loiter. Or but thinly on the void
    Hear our own voices rise. They fall and merge
    In formless music of unlocal surge,
Beating on sorrow's shore for one farewell,
    While from grey sea and sombre heath a dirge
Blows on the heart with solemn, pulsing knell,
Dull, fitful, brief, abrupt, as some snow-muffled bell.

124

And yet death's silence might more fitly robe
  Our sorrow. For the strength of this dear tongue,
Whose large free tones have girdled round the globe,
  Mellowed and subtilized by him who sung
  To his harmonious hearing, lies unstrung
For the full use of grief. The laurels, glossed
  By his warm golden art, whose year was young
And green with winter freshness, now have lost
Life's touch, and droop to dullness, withered in our frost.

125

For song so lived with him, we deemed her wed
  To his one life, whose life itself was song.
And so with her he communed, nought was bred
  But noble issue breathing strength among
  Our sweetened ways. So loyal grew, so strong
His clasp, that something as of nature's rote
  Passed on his spirit. And his love so long,
From his pure privacy of spring would float
Through all our season's dearth a new refreshment's note.

126

And now, by such divorce, if song must die
   With him, or linger widowed and uncrowned,
This were fit passing for true poesy,
   Where love beholdeth, and love's hand hath found
   Fulfilment and farewell in song; where sound
Is not but silence, that his lips may lull
   With their own requiem life, and nature round
   And mellow with her moon, and half annul
By benediction death, and God rise calm and full.

127

Dead? Nay, transfigured, seeing that the mist
   Of life is blown and purgèd by the breath
Cold seeming of that clear idealist,
   Whom his pure spirit's height not needed, death.
   Nay, living, whose dear loss transfigureth
In part, as song in part, and for a space
   O'erpeering sorrow, where it shadoweth
   With its dull brooding vapour, doth efface
Low things, and to his star illumine, lift our race.

128

Leave him, where death's completing touch doth paint
    Round his pale forehead time's last aureole,
And canonize in calm so true a saint
    Of song, who ever held his vision whole,
    Unsoiled; through the pure ether of whose soul,
As one sublimed to listen, set apart,
    God's music wrought and ripened by control
For reconcilement's broad and mellow art,
And beat through nature's bosom to his human heart.

129

No waste is here, no wildness; no dead root
    Of growth misgotten; nought unseasoned, sour,
Decadent, crude; nothing but perfect fruit,
    And calm fulfilment of consummate flower,
    Now falling, at this autumn's frosty hour,
Into the lap of honour, there to live,
    As needing not to wait for death's free power,
Or centuries to winnow in their sieve,
But ripely doth presume timeless prerogative.

130

Perchance I too had laid a fuller wreath,
  To fade or blossom on so high a tomb;
I too, perchance, had seen that soil of death
    Breed from its own pure depth some other bloom
    Than this; had planted there for brief perfume
Some flower of verse, such as I dreamed should blow
    Over song's grave; had followed through the gloom
Of such a twilight time, when song was low,
And stayed his glory's flush, and beauty's afterglow;

131

But that the passion of a death more dear,
  Which circles on me from this central date,
One ripening season of my sorrow's year,
  To its own use doth seal and consecrate
  The yield of all my nature, now too late
For love's fruition; whether it be spring,
  Lent to a spirit quickened to create,
Or winter, which shall nerve anew and string
Myself for lonely growth and life fulfilled to sing.

132

Yet were my sorrow thus a thing too poor
    And private, if I plucked not from the wall
Of love's own home, for song's high sepulture,
    Flushed with the autumn glory of his fall,
    Some leaves of this free speech, imperial
Of England, grave, impassioned; if, aloof,
    I wove not at his passing now a pall
Wrought to our flag's yet full and seamless woof,
Largely to drape his death, under time's solemn roof.

133

Therefore to song's large loss time now shall wed
    My private date of death, that life has wove
Into my spirit's texture; who beheld
    That same sad hour, which hardly breathed above
    His sleeping, steal upon the lips of love,
Which once were mine, with pallid power, and close
    All sweet approach and answer, that might move
With whisper of farewell—as a white rose
Fainting at summer dusk is folded to repose.

134

And therefore consecration's sound hath passed
　On the memory of that mellow sunset song,
Prophetic of his parting, and the last
　Whereto she listened, trembling from my tongue;
　Whose pure waves echoed on, perchance, among
The fragments of her memory, softly stirred
　By little steps, till love, who would prolong
His deepening proof, might ripple with no word
The dreamful shore of death, and only God was heard.

135

And ever shall it haunt this silent room,
　Wherein my lonely spirit doth embalm
All buried sweetness in its love's perfume,
　Mingled for me with what of larger calm
　And sanctity hath fallen on each psalm,
More solemn, by her children's voices read,
　With the faint feeling of her pulseless palm,
Those lilies seen with white and drooping head,
These violets, late for vision, breathing by the dead.

136

There on my heart's white page his lines have writ
    Love's perfect form and creed, which I confess,
The first of his quotation, whence was lit
    In the pure vision of my own princess
    A gleam prophetic, half of doubtfulness,
Half dread that love's allegiance should compel;
    Whence unto mine in slow and sweet accèss,
From the brief magic moment of that spell,
Her lips, her spirit grew, for greeting and farewell.

137

Oh love! Oh death! Would now that I might build
    For memory and for you a monument
Perpetual, pure as his; wherein fulfilled
    My spirit might behold its true ascent,
    And broaden out, perchance, for souls still pent,
In large free service; where I should escape
    Solitude, self, and be for ever blent,
In its most central shrine, with her, and drape
In full and reverent folds my dear love's deathless shape.

138

Were any master mine but doubt and dream,
    Knowledge and nature, loveliness and life,
And she, who woke my spirit with the gleam,
    Wherein all melt and gather—love and wife;
    Were mine an inspiration more than strife
Hath grown, more than begotten was of death,
    And what of passion sane and sweet is rife
In the rich world, and what of reason's breath
Hath blown my nature free, and mingled me with faith;

139

He were, in sooth, the one, whom I had sought,
    To bathe my faculties from the wide brink
Of his pure current, till, perchance, I caught
    Some subtler flow of music; or to drink
    Fuller of memories, which do partly link
His motions unto mine; to raise my pipe
    To rhyme with his large reverent love; or think
Through the deep law, that mouldeth him to type
For me of life and song, things reconciled and ripe.

140

But—for the spirit speaketh what he hath
 Of private vision, things that do belong
To his true thought, and treads a living path
 Only by unattempted streams; and song,
 Set by God's breath, thus slow and late among
New fields, for me has blossomed on the soil
 Of my own nature, freely grown, made strong
By love and death and ripe perfection's toil,
Flowering unfathered, sourceless on the full world's spoil—

141

Now from this lonely tree I were content
 To pluck a leaner fruitage; and to grope
A lower way than his high precedent,
 By my own spirit's clue; if but the slope
 Were sunward; if but seed of golden hope
By me might yet be planted, nutritive,
 Sifted in song, and chosen to the scope
Of time, to whose pure passion love should give
Growth and fulfilment's hour, her law to die to live.

SONG'S SEASON.

ALTHOUGH my lonely year be young
    And timeless still, since death can breed
Some sense of motion from a seed
Planted and slowly grown among
The months, wherein my sorrow sung,
    Since love must flower for living need,
With something of a season's rote
I turn again to nature's note.

Oh crocus, can thy heart of gold,
    Still sleeping hidden in the corm,
    Flame out again and face the storm?
Oh love, for all my winter's cold,
Look forth, and only half unfold,
    In song's new season now, and form
For song, for her, a blossom, though
My heart lie dreaming yet below!

TWO LIVES.

Oh bells of blue, that made a mist,
   Through dull deep green and underwood,
   Breathe, as you breathed upon my mood,
Where no one but the cuckoo wist!
Oh lips of love, which once were kissed,
   When May was waking in the blood,
If dream and shadow yet can sing,
Touch me to listen now for spring!

Oh little lips of tufted thyme,
   Whose silence whispered at her feet
   When summer's passion was complete!
Oh breath of song, who canst not climb
Up to her spirit's height, or rhyme
   With her free motion's beauty, meet
And blend with me and here embalm
Dead sweetness in my spirit's calm!

Oh flush again, thou purple heath,
   This year my nature's solitude,
   And richly colour song's grey mood!
Oh love, who livest warm beneath
My spirit's waste, pulse up from death!
   That with some autumn sense imbued,
My loss may flower to fuller type,
And sorrow's fruit for song be ripe.

TWO LIVES.

Oh plant, whose flowers of lilac pale,
   And leaves of ivy climb and keep
   Life's vision through the month's that sleep!
Oh deathless past, whose tendrils trail
Over my fancy still, and veil
   Its bareness, send your fibres deep
Into my heart, where love once clomb,
And clothe in song love's empty home.

Oh love, to-day, since thou wast born
   In some sweet hour, the date of this,
   I too have felt the sun's light kiss
With earth; for me the woods have worn
Fresh-tasselled catkins, though the thorn
   Be silver yet with clematis;
And by gaunt bracken's withered wraith
The golden gorse has flowered in faith.

Oh song, make thou my seasons one!
   That, shapen for time's true ascent,
   Perchance, in thy prefigurement,
To-morrow's texture, yet unspun,
Inwoven by God's central sun,
   With love and nature purely blent,
May measure by thy mellowing change
My larger growth, my spirit's range.

SOMETHING WHITE.

SOMETHING white! oh is it only foam?
   Is it sail or sea-bird's wing?
Is it brief far vision of the face of home
   Growing on my sense and glistening?
   Am I coming back to England and to spring?

Something white! Has sunny welcome kissed
   Cliff of England, caught between
Yonder grey and edgeless line of lifting mist,
   And this channel's surging sullen green?
   Am I coming back to England and my queen?

Something white! which met me there and smiled
  Was it chestnut's solemn sway?
Was it hawthorn waiting? Was it roses wild
  Stealing summer whilst I was away?
  Am I coming back to England and to May?

Something white! Oh full Venetian moon,
  Is it still thy mellow gleam
On canal and campanile and lagune,
  Moving with me down my memory's stream?
  Am I coming back to England out of dream?

Something white! Ah, was it snow of Greece?
  Proud Parnassus set among
Purple mountains, sea of sapphire, with his peace
  Haunting my o'ertravelled sense, how long?
  Am I coming back to England and to song?

Something white! Oh, that was long ago.
  Shining there beyond, above
Cliff of England, sweetness on me seemed to grow,

Something from spring's whitest blossoms wove;
I was coming back to England and to love.

Something white! Oh is it sorrow's wing
   Wafted back on song's own breath?
Is it love's fair blossom fallen, withering,
   Blown about dead passion for a wreath?
   Am I coming back to England and to death?

Something white! Oh is it bridal bloom?
   Is it love on sorrow grown?
Broadening, blending with a fresh and full perfume
   Through a people's soul and round a throne?
   Am I coming back to England, and alone?

Something white! Oh pure and full and far,
   Thou art waiting, love, for me,
For my song's true season, still my living star,
   Blent with love of England, one and free,
   I am coming back to England and to thee.

Something white! For me love flowered here;
    Here my love shall grow and sing,
Clasping summer hope to memory's fruitful year,
    Nevermore a dead and lonely thing;
    I am coming back to England and to spring.

CHISWICK PRESS:—C. WHITTINGHAM AND CO., TOOKS COURT, CHANCERY LANE.

www.ingramcontent.com/pod-product-compliance
Lightning Source LLC
Chambersburg PA
CBHW020900230426
43666CB00008B/1251